75 Caramelizing Recipes

(75 Caramelizing Recipes - Volume 1)

Maria Bingham

Copyright: Published in the United States by Maria Bingham/ © MARIA BINGHAM

Published on December, 11 2020

All rights reserved. No part of this publication may be reproduced, stored in retrieval system, copied in any form or by any means, electronic, mechanical, photocopying, recording or otherwise transmitted without written permission from the publisher. Please do not participate in or encourage piracy of this material in any way. You must not circulate this book in any format. MARIA BINGHAM does not control or direct users' actions and is not responsible for the information or content shared, harm and/or actions of the book readers.

In accordance with the U.S. Copyright Act of 1976, the scanning, uploading and electronic sharing of any part of this book without the permission of the publisher constitute unlawful piracy and theft of the author's intellectual property. If you would like to use material from the book (other than just simply for reviewing the book), prior permission must be obtained by contacting the author at author@thymerecipes.com

Thank you for your support of the author's rights.

Content

75 AWESOME CARAMELIZING RECIPES 5

1. Apricot Tarte Tatin 5
2. Baked Banana With Poppy Seed Honey Ice Cream And Chocolate Tuiles 5
3. Blood Oranges With Red Wine 7
4. Braised Chicken Thighs With Caramelized Fennel 7
5. Brooks Headley's Ice Cream Sandwich 8
6. Buckwheat Harvest Tart 8
7. Burnt Oranges With Rosemary 9
8. Burnt Sugar Ice Cream With Butterscotch Sauce 10
9. Burrata With Bacon, Escarole And Caramelized Shallots 11
10. Butternut Squash, Caramelized Onion And Spinach Lasagna 11
11. Calf's Liver With Grapes 12
12. Caramel Cake 13
13. Caramel Glazed Pears 14
14. Caramel Pudding With Chex Streusel 14
15. Caramel Syrup 15
16. Caramelized Baked Apples 16
17. Caramelized Brown Butter Rice Krispies Treats 16
18. Caramelized Citrus 17
19. Caramelized Figs With Honey, Thyme And Crème Fraîche 17
20. Caramelized Onion Dip With Frizzled Leeks 18
21. Caramelized Onion And Lentil Pilaf 19
22. Caramelized Onion And Mushroom Matzo Brei 19
23. Caramelized Peaches 20
24. Charlotte Aux Poires William Et Caramel 20
25. Chicken Livers With Caramelized Onions And Mushrooms 21
26. Clay Pot Pork 22
27. Coconut Dulce De Leche With Caramelized Pineapple 23
28. Curried Spinach Stuffing With Caramelized Onions 23
29. Dried Fruit And Nut Bsteeyas 24
30. Duck Or Rabbit Livers With Onion Marmalade 25
31. Endive Cheese Tart 25
32. English Pea And Onion Salad 26
33. Florence Fabricant's Praline 27
34. Foolproof Tarte Tatin 27
35. Glazed Mango With Sour Cream Sorbet And Black Pepper 28
36. Grilled Peach Sundaes With Salted Bourbon Caramel Sauce 29
37. Hete Bliksem 29
38. Honey Apple Pie With Thyme 30
39. Irish Cream Caramel Sauce 31
40. Irish Oatmeal Brulee With Dried Fruit And Maple Cream 31
41. Linguine With Crab Meat 32
42. Maple Sugar Creme Caramel 33
43. Matzo Brei With Caramelized Apples 33
44. Pasta With Caramelized Onion, Swiss Chard And Garlicky Bread Crumbs 34
45. Pasta With Fried Lemons And Chile Flakes 35
46. Peach Upside Down Skillet Cake With Bourbon Whipped Cream 36
47. Peaches In Amaretto Caramel 37
48. Peanut Brittle 37
49. Pear Pomegranate Pie 38
50. Pineapples Victoria 38
51. Pizza With Caramelized Onions, Figs, Bacon And Blue Cheese 39
52. Pizza With Caramelized Onions, Ricotta And Chard 40
53. Pizza With Spring Onions And Fennel 41
54. Praline 41
55. Praline Pear Cake 42
56. Provençal Onion Pizza 42
57. Pumpkin Flan 43
58. Rawia Bishara's Vegetarian Musaqa 44
59. Rhineland Sauerbraten 45
60. Rigatoni And Cauliflower Al Forno 47
61. Roasted Blood Oranges 47
62. Roseanne Gold's Pumpkin Flan 48
63. Salted Butter Caramels 48
64. Sausage Ragù 49
65. Seared Albacore And Peaches With Quinoa, Haricots Verts And Pistou 50
66. Seared Scallops With Hot Sauce Beurre Blanc 51

67. Singaporean Braised Duck 52
68. Sliced Oranges With Pomegranate Caramelized Walnuts 52
69. Smoked Trout In Caramelized Apple And Onion Broth 53
70. Spiced Caramel Syrup 54
71. Spiced Pumpkin Creme Brulee With Ginger Dusted Churros 54
72. Spicy Spaghetti With Caramelized Onions And Herbs 55
73. Sweet Potato Soup 55
74. Thyme Meringue Cookies With Boozy Apple 56
75. Vidalia Onion Soup With Wild Rice And Maytag Blue Cheese Croutons 57

INDEX **58**

CONCLUSION **61**

75 Awesome Caramelizing Recipes

***

1. Apricot Tarte Tatin

Serving: 6 to 8 servings | Prep: | Cook: | Ready in: 45mins

Ingredients

- For the pastry:
- 1 cup unbleached all-purpose flour
- 6 tablespoons cold unsalted butter cut into small pieces
- 1 teaspoon sugar
- A pinch of salt
- About 2 tablespoons ice water
- For the apricots:
- 2 pounds apricots
- 2 tablespoons unsalted butter
- ½ cup sugar

Direction

- Make the pastry. In a food processor, combine the flour, butter, sugar and salt. Process until the mixture looks like coarse bread crumbs (about five seconds). Add the cold water and process briefly, turning the machine on and off, until the mixture looks like small peas. Do not allow to become a ball in the machine.
- Turn mixture out onto lightly floured board and knead lightly until it holds together. With heel of palm of your hand, flatten it into a thick pancake about six inches across. Wrap it in plastic and refrigerate for at least 20 minutes. It will keep unfrozen up to three days before being used.
- Cut apricots in half and remove pits. Melt butter and sugar in nine-inch cast-iron skillet. Arrange apricot halves in circles on top and cook over moderate heat, without burning, until sugar begins to caramelize. Be careful not to burn. Cool completely.
- Roll out pastry into 10-inch circle. Place it on top of apricots, cutting off excess dough. Put edges down over fruit. Refrigerate for 30 minutes.
- Preheat oven to 425 degrees.
- Prick the pastry all over with the point of a knife. Bake for 20 to 25 minutes until the pastry is cooked.
- Cool and turn out onto a plate. Do not be dismayed if some of the apricots stick to pan; simply scrape them off and put them on top of pastry.

Nutrition Information

- 264: calories;
- 38 grams: carbohydrates;
- 24 grams: sugars;
- 40 milligrams: sodium;
- 7 grams: saturated fat;
- 0 grams: trans fat;
- 3 grams: protein;
- 1 gram: polyunsaturated fat;
- 12 grams: fat;

2. Baked Banana With Poppy Seed Honey Ice Cream And Chocolate Tuiles

Serving: 6 servings | Prep: | Cook: | Ready in: 1hours

Ingredients

- For the ice cream:

- 6 large egg yolks
- 2 cups milk
- ½ cup heavy cream
- ⅓ cup honey
- Pinch of salt
- 2 tablespoons poppy seeds
- For the tuiles:
- ½ cup sugar
- 3 tablespoons cocoa powder
- 3 tablespoons flour
- 1 ½ ounces bittersweet chocolate
- 3 tablespoons light corn syrup
- 2 tablespoons unsalted butter
- 2 tablespoons water
- For the bananas:
- ½ cup sugar
- 2 tablespoons water
- 7 tablespoons heavy cream
- 6 tablespoons unsalted butter
- 6 bananas, unpeeled

Direction

- To make the ice cream, place the yolks in a large bowl and whisk until smooth. Place the milk, cream, honey and salt in a saucepan and bring just to a boil. Remove from heat and slowly whisk the hot liquid into the yolks. Whisk in the poppy seeds. Refrigerate until chilled, and freeze according to the instructions for your ice-cream maker.
- To make the tuiles, place the sugar, cocoa and flour in a small bowl and whisk them together. Place the chocolate, corn syrup, butter and water in the top of a double boiler set over simmering water and cook, stirring occasionally, until smooth. While the butter-and-chocolate mixture is still warm, combine it with the dry ingredients, and stir until smooth.
- Preheat the oven to 300 degrees. On a nonstick cookie sheet, drop a little less than a tablespoon of the batter, and use a small spatula to spread it into a circle 3 1/2 inches in diameter. Continue until you have 3 cookies formed, leaving at least 1 inch between each. Bake until the cookies are bubbly and lacy, 6 to 8 minutes. Remove from the oven and cool on the pan for 1 minute. Use a spatula to loosen the cookies from the pan and transfer them to a wire rack to cool. Continue to form and bake the cookies until you have about 12 good-looking ones. Set aside. (Once cool, the cookies may be stored in an air-tight container until needed.)
- To make the bananas, place the sugar and water in a heavy saucepan set over medium heat and bring to a boil. Continue to cook until the mixture turns a deep amber color. Immediately turn off the heat and carefully add the cream. (The mixture will sputter.) Stir in the butter. Transfer mixture to a bowl, and refrigerate until ready to use.
- When ready to serve, preheat the oven to 350 degrees. With a sharp knife, cut out a wedge from each banana that runs almost its entire length, and keep the peel attached at one end. Remove and discard the flesh portions of each wedge and fill the resulting cavity with the caramel sauce. Transfer the bananas to a baking sheet lined with aluminum foil, and bake until very soft, about 20 minutes.
- Transfer the warm bananas to serving plates, and place a tuile on each plate. Scoop the ice cream onto the tuile, and garnish with yet another piece of tuile, standing it upright in the ice cream like a flag.

Nutrition Information

- 759: calories;
- 1 gram: trans fat;
- 99 grams: carbohydrates;
- 81 grams: sugars;
- 9 grams: protein;
- 119 milligrams: sodium;
- 40 grams: fat;
- 23 grams: saturated fat;
- 3 grams: polyunsaturated fat;
- 5 grams: dietary fiber;
- 12 grams: monounsaturated fat;

3. Blood Oranges With Red Wine

Serving: 4 to 6 servings | Prep: | Cook: | Ready in: 45mins

Ingredients

- 12 blood oranges
- ½ cup sugar
- 3 tablespoons water
- ½ cup dry red wine
- Mint sprigs

Direction

- Peel the oranges, removing all the white pith. Separate them into sections and place in a bowl.
- Dissolve the sugar in the water in a shallow saucepan. Place over medium-high heat and cook, swirling the mixture from time to time, until it becomes honey colored. Remove from the heat. Pour in the wine, standing back from the pan because it may spatter. Stir briefly so all the caramel dissolves in the wine.
- Pour over the oranges and chill until ready to serve.
- Serve in goblets decorated with mint sprigs.

Nutrition Information

- 204: calories;
- 0 grams: polyunsaturated fat;
- 48 grams: carbohydrates;
- 6 grams: dietary fiber;
- 41 grams: sugars;
- 2 grams: protein;
- 1 milligram: sodium;

4. Braised Chicken Thighs With Caramelized Fennel

Serving: 4 servings | Prep: | Cook: | Ready in: 45mins

Ingredients

- 2 large fennel bulbs
- 1 large clove garlic, roughly chopped
- ½ teaspoon grated lemon zest
- 1 teaspoon kosher salt
- ⅓ cup plus 2 tablespoons extra virgin olive oil
- 6 boneless chicken thighs (about 1 1/4 pounds)
- ½ teaspoon ground black pepper
- ½ teaspoon fennel seeds
- 1 onion, thinly sliced
- 1 tablespoon Pernod
- 1 tablespoon freshly squeezed lemon juice

Direction

- Trim fennel bulbs, and set aside fronds. In a blender or food processor, pulse about 1/2 cup fronds, garlic, lemon zest and 1/4 teaspoon salt until finely chopped. Add 1/3 cup oil and purée.
- Halve fennel bulbs lengthwise. Slice thinly with a mandoline or very sharp knife.
- Season chicken with 1/2 teaspoon salt and 1/4 teaspoon pepper. Heat remaining 2 tablespoons oil in a large skillet over high heat. Brown chicken until skin is crisp, about 8 minutes. Transfer chicken to a plate, leaving drippings in pan.
- Stir fennel seeds into skillet and cook for 30 seconds. Add sliced fennel and onion, seasoning with remaining 1/4 teaspoon salt and 1/4 teaspoon pepper. Reduce heat to medium and cook, tossing occasionally, until vegetables are caramelized, 15 to 20 minutes. Add Pernod and scrape up any browned bits in the bottom of the skillet; cook until liquid has evaporated, about 1 minute.
- Lay chicken on top of the fennel-onion mixture. Pour 3 tablespoons water into the pan. Cover skillet and reduce heat to medium-low. Cook until chicken is just cooked through, 8 to 10 minutes. Uncover and cook off any excess liquid if necessary. Stir in lemon juice.

- Serve chicken and vegetables topped with generous dollops of the fennel frond purée.

Nutrition Information

- 507: calories;
- 42 grams: fat;
- 0 grams: trans fat;
- 5 grams: dietary fiber;
- 7 grams: sugars;
- 19 grams: protein;
- 629 milligrams: sodium;
- 8 grams: saturated fat;
- 25 grams: monounsaturated fat;
- 6 grams: polyunsaturated fat;
- 15 grams: carbohydrates;

5. Brooks Headley's Ice Cream Sandwich

Serving: 4 servings | Prep: | Cook: | Ready in: 10mins

Ingredients

- 2 slices white bread (preferably Pepperidge Farm)
- 1 cup gelato or ice cream (of your preference, but the author suggests Ben & Jerry's Cherry Garcia), softened but not melting
- 1 teaspoon unsalted butter
- Coarse sea salt
- Extra-virgin olive oil

Direction

- Smear the bread with butter and sear in a cast-iron or nonstick pan until lightly caramelized and golden. Allow to cool a few minutes. Place the bread sear-side out on a work surface. Scoop the gelato onto one slice of bread and top with the other slice. Slice into 4 pieces and top with a drizzle with high quality extra-virgin olive oil and a light sprinkle of salt. Serve immediately, or hold in the freezer for up to one hour.

Nutrition Information

- 121: calories;
- 3 grams: protein;
- 1 gram: dietary fiber;
- 115 milligrams: sodium;
- 2 grams: monounsaturated fat;
- 15 grams: carbohydrates;
- 8 grams: sugars;
- 6 grams: fat;
- 0 grams: polyunsaturated fat;

6. Buckwheat Harvest Tart

Serving: 6 servings | Prep: | Cook: | Ready in: 2hours30mins

Ingredients

- For the crust
- 1 cup buckwheat flour
- ¾ cup unbleached all-purpose flour
- ½ teaspoon sea salt
- ½ cup cold unsalted butter, cut into cubes
- 2 teaspoons fresh thyme leaves
- 1 tablespoon apple cider vinegar
- 2 to 3 tablespoons cold water
- For the filling
- 3 cups cubed butternut squash (1/4-inch cubes)
- 2 tablespoons extra virgin olive oil
- Sea salt and freshly ground black pepper
- ½ teaspoon freshly grated nutmeg
- 2 cloves garlic, minced
- 1 bunch Swiss chard, stems removed, coarsely chopped (about 6 cups chopped)
- ½ teaspoon red pepper flakes
- 1 small yellow onion
- 2 tablespoons balsamic vinegar
- 3 eggs
- 1 cup grated Gruyère

Direction

- To make the crust: In a food processor, add both flours and the salt and pulse to combine. Add the butter and thyme and pulse until pea-size chunks form. Keep pulsing while adding the vinegar and then the cold water, 1 tablespoon at a time, stopping when the dough just barely holds together. Form the dough into a disk, wrap it in plastic wrap and chill in the fridge for at least 30 minutes or up to overnight.
- Preheat oven to 400 degrees.
- On a lightly floured surface, roll out the dough into a 13-inch circle. It should be about 1/4 inch thick. Roll the dough around the rolling pin and lift it into an 11-inch fluted tart pan with a removable bottom. Press the dough into the edges and up the sides, making sure to patch up any holes. Gently roll your rolling pin across the top of the tart pan to remove the extra dough and create a clean edge. Prick the bottom of the dough with a fork, lay a piece of parchment paper on top, and fill the tart shell with pie weights (at the Sprouted Kitchen, we use rocks from the yard — classy, I know). Bake for 15 minutes. Remove the weights and parchment, and bake until the top looks almost dry, 10 to 12 minutes more. Remove from the oven and let cool.
- While the crust is cooling, prepare the filling. On a rimmed baking sheet, toss the squash with 1/2 tablespoon of the olive oil, 1/2 teaspoon salt and the nutmeg. Spread in an even layer and bake until the squash begins to brown around the edges, 20 to 25 minutes. Remove from the oven and let cool.
- In a large sauté pan over medium heat, warm 1 tablespoon of the olive oil and the garlic. When the garlic starts to sizzle a bit and becomes fragrant, add the Swiss chard, red pepper flakes and a pinch of salt. Sauté until the chard is wilted, about 5 minutes. Transfer to a large mixing bowl and set aside.
- Peel and halve the onion and thinly slice. In the same pan you used for the chard, heat the remaining 1/2 tablespoon olive oil over medium heat. Add the onion and a pinch of salt and stir every so often until it is caramelized, about 20 minutes. When the onions are a nice light brown color, add the balsamic vinegar, stir and turn off the heat. The onions will absorb the vinegar as they cool a bit.
- Squeeze out any excess water from the Swiss chard and return to the bowl. In a separate bowl, whisk the eggs until they are blended well, then add to the chard. To the bowl with the chard, add three-fourths of the squash, half of the cheese, the onion and a few grinds of black pepper. Gently mix everything together and pour into the tart pan. Spread into an even layer. Scatter the remaining squash and cheese across the top. Bake in the oven until the egg is just set and the top is browned, 24 to 28 minutes. Remove the tart from the oven and allow it to cool for 5 to 10 minutes before cutting into slices and serving.

Nutrition Information

- 482: calories;
- 1 gram: trans fat;
- 11 grams: monounsaturated fat;
- 2 grams: polyunsaturated fat;
- 40 grams: carbohydrates;
- 16 grams: protein;
- 30 grams: fat;
- 15 grams: saturated fat;
- 6 grams: dietary fiber;
- 4 grams: sugars;
- 642 milligrams: sodium;

7. Burnt Oranges With Rosemary

Serving: 4 servings | Prep: | Cook: | Ready in: 4mins

Ingredients

- 4 oranges, halved, peeled, pith removed
- 2 tablespoons fresh rosemary

- ½ cup sugar
- 1 cup plain thick Greek yogurt

Direction

- Place oranges cut-side up on a plate and sprinkle rosemary on top, pressing it into oranges so it adheres. Sprinkle with 1/4 cup sugar.
- On a grill or stovetop, put a 12-inch cast iron skillet over medium heat until a drop of water sizzles on surface. Spread remaining 1/4 cup sugar in skillet and when it starts to caramelize place oranges, cut-side down, on sugar. Let cook for 3 to 4 minutes, not moving oranges, so cut side burns nicely and oranges soften.
- To serve, place 2 orange halves in bowl with 1/4 cup Greek yogurt, and drizzle with burnt sugar juices from skillet.

Nutrition Information

- 222: calories;
- 4 grams: fat;
- 34 milligrams: sodium;
- 2 grams: saturated fat;
- 0 grams: polyunsaturated fat;
- 43 grams: carbohydrates;
- 3 grams: dietary fiber;
- 40 grams: sugars;
- 7 grams: protein;

8. Burnt Sugar Ice Cream With Butterscotch Sauce

Serving: 6 to 8 servings | Prep: | Cook: | Ready in: 40mins

Ingredients

- The ice cream:
- 2 cups milk
- 1 large egg
- ¼ cup flour
- 1 cup sugar
- 1 ½ tablespoons finely grated orange rind
- 1 cup heavy cream
- The butterscotch sauce:
- 1 ½ cups sugar
- 1 ½ cups light corn syrup
- ¼ cup butter
- ⅔ cup heavy cream
- ¼ cup bourbon

Direction

- Pour the milk into a saucepan, and bring to a simmer.
- Combine the egg, flour and 1/2 cup of the sugar in the bowl of an electric mixer. Start beating the mixture until it is thoroughly blended, and pour in the hot milk. Pour and scrape the sauce into a saucepan, and start beating over moderate heat. Cook until the mixture is thickened and smooth.
- Put the remaining 1/2 cup of sugar into a small nonstick skillet, and cook, stirring, until the sugar is melted and starts to take on a light caramel color. Immediately add the orange rind, and blend, stirring constantly. Remove from the heat. Immediately add the caramel-orange mixture to the sauce and blend.
- Line a mixing bowl with a sieve, and pour the sauce into it, pressing all around with the sides of a rubber spatula to extract as much flavor as possible from the orange rind. Discard the rind.
- Add the 1 cup of heavy cream, and stir. Let cool. Pour the mixture into the container of a hand-cranked or electric ice cream maker, and freeze according to the manufacturer's instructions.
- Meanwhile, to prepare the butterscotch sauce, put the 1 1/2 cups of sugar into a 12-inch nonstick skillet, and cook, stirring, until the sugar is melted and becomes a dark caramel in color. Add the corn syrup, stir to blend, and remove from the heat. Stir in the butter to blend. Stir in the 2/3 cup of cream and the

bourbon. Spoon the sauce over the ice cream and serve.

Nutrition Information

- 724: calories;
- 16 grams: saturated fat;
- 8 grams: monounsaturated fat;
- 1 gram: polyunsaturated fat;
- 119 grams: carbohydrates;
- 95 milligrams: sodium;
- 27 grams: fat;
- 0 grams: dietary fiber;
- 116 grams: sugars;
- 4 grams: protein;

9. Burrata With Bacon, Escarole And Caramelized Shallots

Serving: 12 servings | Prep: | Cook: | Ready in: 1hours30mins

Ingredients

- For the cooking the escarole
- ¾ cup extra virgin olive oil
- 6 garlic cloves, chopped
- 1 shallot, chopped
- 2 medium heads escarole (about 1 1/4 pounds)
- 2 teaspoons kosher salt
- For the caramelized shallots
- 3 tablespoons extra virgin olive oil
- 1 ⅓ cups thinly sliced lengthwise shallots (about 6 to 8)
- ¼ cup plus 2 tablespoons balsamic vinegar
- For the dressing the escarole
- 1 cup minced shallots (about 4)
- ¼ cup Champagne vinegar, or to taste
- 1 large garlic clove, minced
- 1 ½ teaspoons kosher salt, or to taste
- ¼ cup extra virgin olive oil, or to taste
- For the finishing and assembly

- 12 slices of batard, fat baguette or rustic white bread, 1/2-inch thick
- Extra virgin olive oil, as needed
- 12 thick slices (about 12 ounces) smoked bacon
- 2 garlic cloves
- 1 ½ pounds burrata
- Extra virgin olive oil
- Coarsely ground pepper

Direction

-
-

Nutrition Information

- 661: calories;
- 29 grams: monounsaturated fat;
- 26 grams: carbohydrates;
- 4 grams: dietary fiber;
- 703 milligrams: sodium;
- 53 grams: fat;
- 15 grams: saturated fat;
- 0 grams: trans fat;
- 6 grams: polyunsaturated fat;
- 7 grams: sugars;
- 21 grams: protein;

10. Butternut Squash, Caramelized Onion And Spinach Lasagna

Serving: 8 to 10 servings | Prep: | Cook: | Ready in: 3hours15mins

Ingredients

- 1 large butternut squash
- 6 tablespoons olive oil, divided
- 3 red onions, medium, julienned
- 1 pound part-skim ricotta cheese
- 2 tablespoons rosemary, chopped
- 2 eggs
- 1 ½ cups grated Parmesan cheese, divided
- 3 tablespoons unsalted butter

- Scant 1/2 cup all-purpose flour
- 3 ½ cups whole milk
- Pinch nutmeg
- 1 bag chopped frozen spinach (1-pound), defrosted and drained
- 6 sheets fresh pasta, or no-boil lasagna noodles
- Salt
- Pepper

Direction

- Roast the butternut squash. Preheat oven to 375 degrees. Cut squash in half lengthwise; remove seeds. Place in roasting pan and drizzle with 3 tablespoons of olive oil. Place in oven and cook until soft all the way through, about 1 hour. Set aside until cool. When cooled, remove skin and place in food processor. Purée until smooth, season with salt and pepper to taste, and set aside.
- To caramelize the onions: Place 3 tablespoons of olive oil in sauté pan. Heat until hot but not smoking; add onions. Toss to coat with oil. Turn heat down to medium and cook until onions are soft and browned, about 25 minutes. Season with salt and pepper to taste. Set aside.
- Prepare a ricotta cheese mixture. Mix ricotta cheese, chopped rosemary, eggs, half the grated Parmesan and salt and pepper to taste. Set aside.
- Make a spinach Mornay sauce. Melt butter in a saucepan, add flour and stir. Cook 2 minutes. Add milk and stir until it comes to a boil. Add the rest of the grated Parmesan, the nutmeg and the defrosted spinach. Season with salt and pepper. Set aside.
- Assemble the dish. Spray a 9" x 13" pan with cooking spray. Spread 1 cup of the spinach sauce on the bottom of the pan. Cover with a layer of fresh pasta sheets. Spread half of the roasted butternut squash on top of the pasta sheets. Top with another layer of pasta sheets. Spread ricotta cheese mixture on top of pasta sheets, and spread caramelized onion on top of ricotta mixture. Cover with an additional layer of pasta sheets. Top with the other half of the butternut purée and then another layer of pasta. Finish by using the rest of the spinach Mornay sauce for the top layer. Cover with aluminum foil and bake at 350 degrees for 1 hour. Uncover and cook for 15 minutes more.

Nutrition Information

- 436: calories;
- 8 grams: sugars;
- 20 grams: protein;
- 0 grams: trans fat;
- 2 grams: polyunsaturated fat;
- 33 grams: carbohydrates;
- 3 grams: dietary fiber;
- 790 milligrams: sodium;
- 26 grams: fat;
- 12 grams: saturated fat;
- 11 grams: monounsaturated fat;

11. Calf's Liver With Grapes

Serving: 4 servings | Prep: | Cook: | Ready in: 20mins

Ingredients

- 8 thin slices calf's liver, about 1 1/2 pounds
- Salt to taste if desired
- Freshly ground pepper to taste
- ⅓ cup flour
- 1 tablespoon sugar
- 1 tablespoon red-wine vinegar
- 1 cup fresh or canned chicken broth
- 1 tablespoon tomato paste
- 1 ½ cups red or white seedless grapes
- 3 tablespoons butter
- 3 to 4 tablespoons corn, peanut or vegetable oil

Direction

- Sprinkle liver on both sides with salt and pepper.
- Dip pieces in flour to coat well on both sides. Shake off excess. Set aside.

- Combine sugar and vinegar in heavy saucepan and bring to boil. Cook, shaking saucepan and stirring, until liquid evaporates. Continue cooking until sugar becomes caramel color. Take care that it does not burn.
- Add chicken broth and stir in tomato paste. Bring to boil and cook 5 minutes or longer until reduced to 1/2 cup. Add grapes and butter.
- Heat 2 tablespoons of oil in heavy skillet and when hot add pieces of liver, a few at a time, in one layer. Cook 1 or 2 minutes on one side and turn. Cooking time will depend on thickness. Cook on second side 1 or 2 minutes. As pieces are cooked transfer to heated platter. Continue adding pieces and a little more oil to skillet as necessary, tablespoon at a time.
- Bring sauce to boil and pour onto liver. Serve with mashed potatoes or pureed cauliflower (see recipe).

Nutrition Information

- 388: calories;
- 17 grams: protein;
- 25 grams: carbohydrates;
- 8 grams: saturated fat;
- 3 grams: polyunsaturated fat;
- 1 gram: dietary fiber;
- 12 grams: monounsaturated fat;
- 13 grams: sugars;
- 555 milligrams: sodium;

12. Caramel Cake

Serving: One layer cake | Prep: | Cook: | Ready in: 1hours30mins

Ingredients

- For the cake
- 1 cup softened butter, plus more to grease pans
- 3 cups cake flour
- 1 teaspoon baking powder
- ½ teaspoon salt
- 2 cups sugar
- 4 eggs, well beaten
- 1 teaspoon vanilla
- 1 cup milk
- For the icing
- 2 ½ cups sugar
- 8 tablespoons butter
- ½ cup heavy cream
- ¼ teaspoon kosher salt
- 2 teaspoons vanilla
- 1 teaspoon baking soda

Direction

- Preheat oven to 350 degrees. Grease three 9-inch cake pans and line with rounds of parchment or waxed paper.
- Sift flour, then sift again with baking powder and salt. In a mixer, cream together butter and sugar until fluffy, about three minutes. Beat in eggs one at a time and continue to mix on medium until eggs are well incorporated. Stir in vanilla.
- With the mixer on low, alternately add flour and milk, then increase speed to medium. Beat until smooth, about four or five minutes, scraping down sides of bowl.
- Fill each pan about three-quarters full with batter. Bake 20 to 25 minutes or until cake springs lightly when pressed with a finger. Flip cake out of pan onto paper towels or cake rack while still very warm.
- When layers go into oven, start to make icing. Put a half-cup sugar in a large cast-iron pan and set over medium-high heat, stirring until sugar melts and begins to turn dark brown. Be careful not to let it burn. Remove pan from heat.
- Add butter, cream, remaining sugar and salt. Over medium-high heat, bring to a boil and cook for three minutes, stirring, until it reaches about 240 degrees on a candy thermometer.
- Remove from heat and add vanilla and baking soda. Using an electric hand mixer, beat until the icing is spreadable and fluffy. Frost tops of

each layer immediately, stack and then frost sides of cake.

13. Caramel Glazed Pears

Serving: 4 servings | Prep: | Cook: | Ready in: 1hours15mins

Ingredients

- For the pears:
- 6 cups fruity white wine, like Riesling (about 1 1/2 bottles)
- 1 vanilla bean
- 2 strips lemon rind
- 4 Bosc pears
- For the glaze:
- 2 cups sugar
- 1 cup water
- About 1 cup creme fraiche

Direction

- Combine the wine, vanilla bean and lemon rind in a large saucepan. Peel the pears carefully with a vegetable peeler and pull out the blossom end with the tip of the peeler so the pears will be able to stand up. Leave the stem attached. As you peel the pears, drop them in the wine.
- Bring the wine to simmer and cook the pears until they are tender but not mushy, about 30 to 40 minutes. Remove the pears from the syrup and set them aside. Boil poaching liquid to a fourth of a cup.
- Stand the pears up on a baking sheet. Fill a shallow pan with cold water for cooling the caramel and set aside.
- Heat the sugar and one cup of water in a small saucepan without stirring until it turns a deep honey color. Remove the saucepan from the heat and dip the bottom in the pan of cold water to stop the caramel from coloring any further. Pour the hot caramel over each pear, covering it completely. If the caramel hardens while you are working, reheat it.
- Place a spoonful of poaching liquid on each of four plates. Top with a pear and garnish with a dollop of creme fraiche.

Nutrition Information

- 857: calories;
- 6 grams: dietary fiber;
- 140 grams: carbohydrates;
- 124 grams: sugars;
- 2 grams: protein;
- 46 milligrams: sodium;
- 11 grams: fat;
- 3 grams: monounsaturated fat;
- 0 grams: polyunsaturated fat;

14. Caramel Pudding With Chex Streusel

Serving: 12 servings | Prep: | Cook: | Ready in: 1hours

Ingredients

- For the Budino:
- 1 cup/220 grams brown sugar
- ¼ cup/60 milliliters corn syrup
- 3 cups/720 milliliters heavy cream
- 1 ½ cups/360 milliliters whole milk
- 1 vanilla bean, halved and seeds scraped
- 1 large egg, plus 3 large yolks
- 5 tablespoons/40 grams cornstarch
- ½ teaspoon salt, more to taste
- 5 tablespoons/70 grams butter, cubed
- 2 tablespoons/30 milliliters whiskey, preferably High West Double Rye (optional)
- For the Chex Topping:
- ¼ box/85 grams Chex cereal
- ½ cup/110 grams brown sugar
- ½ cup/113 grams unsalted butter, melted
- ½ cup/63 grams all-purpose flour
- ½ teaspoon/1 gram ground cinnamon

- ½ teaspoon/3 milliliters vanilla extract
- Salt and freshly grated nutmeg, to taste
- For the Maple Whipped Mascarpone:
- 1 cup/240 milliliters heavy cream
- 1 cup/226 grams mascarpone cheese
- 1 cup/240 milliliters maple syrup
- Sea salt, to taste

Direction

- Make the budino: Combine brown sugar, corn syrup and 2 tablespoons water in a large heavy pot. Set over medium heat and cook, stirring, until mixture is smooth and sugar begins to caramelize, about 3 minutes.
- Add cream, milk and the vanilla bean pod and seeds and continue cooking over medium heat, stirring often, until sugar is dissolved, about 8 minutes.
- In a large bowl, whisk together whole egg, egg yolks and cornstarch. Very slowly, add 1/2 cup of the hot cream mixture, whisking constantly. Pour tempered egg mixture into pot, whisking constantly to keep eggs from scrambling. Cook 6 to 8 more minutes, stirring constantly, until mixture is thick. Remove from heat and discard vanilla bean.
- Add salt, butter and whiskey. Emulsify budino with an immersion hand blender, or transfer to a regular blender and pulse until butter is melted and incorporated. Taste and add salt, if desired.
- Working quickly so a skin does not form, pour budino into 12 4-ounce ramekins or small jars. Let cool in the refrigerator until set, about 4 hours.
- Meanwhile, make the Chex topping: Heat oven to 350 degrees. Mix Chex, brown sugar, butter, flour, cinnamon, vanilla, salt and nutmeg in a large bowl until cereal is coated. Spread mixture on a parchment-lined baking sheet and bake 20 minutes, tossing every 5 minutes, until browned and crisp. Let cool.
- Make the whipped mascarpone: Beat cream with an electric mixer on medium-high speed until soft peaks form. Add mascarpone and maple syrup and beat on medium speed until smooth. Season with salt, then transfer to a piping bag. Pipe whipped cheese on top of set budinos. Sprinkle Chex on top.

Nutrition Information

- 731: calories;
- 50 grams: fat;
- 14 grams: monounsaturated fat;
- 68 grams: carbohydrates;
- 5 grams: protein;
- 529 milligrams: sodium;
- 31 grams: saturated fat;
- 1 gram: dietary fiber;
- 2 grams: polyunsaturated fat;
- 53 grams: sugars;

15. Caramel Syrup

Serving: 2 - 2 1/2 cups | Prep: | Cook: |Ready in: 35mins

Ingredients

- 3 cups sugar
- ½ cup cold water
- ½ teaspoon lemon juice

Direction

- Combine sugar and water in a heavy-bottom saucepan made of stainless steel, aluminum, copper or unchipped agate. Start cooking over low heat. If any syrup spatters onto the inside of the saucepan, use a brush dipped in cold water to wipe it away. This will prevent the syrup from crystallizing when it has finished cooking.
- Once syrup is boiling, add lemon juice. Continue cooking until syrup has a clear dark-amber or caramel color. It should register about 248 degrees on a thermometer used for candy. It will take about 20 minutes for the syrup to start to boil.

Nutrition Information

- 387: calories;
- 0 grams: protein;
- 100 grams: sugars;
- 2 milligrams: sodium;

16. Caramelized Baked Apples

Serving: 10 servings | Prep: | Cook: | Ready in: 45mins

Ingredients

- The apples:
- 10 medium-large firm apples, such as Cortland, Rome or Ida Red
- Zest of 1 small lemon, grated
- 1 ½ cups fresh apple cider
- 1 tablespoon vegetable oil
- The caramel:
- 2 cups sugar
- The accompaniment:
- 1 ½ cups heavy cream
- 3 tablespoons crystalized ginger, cut into fine dice

Direction

- Preheat the oven to 375 degrees.
- Wash and core to a half-inch of the bottoms of each apple. With a vegetable peeler, peel the tops and bottoms of each apple, leaving a band of skin approximately two inches wide. Place the apples one to two inches apart in a large baking dish. Sprinkle a little of the zest into the well of each apple. Add the cider to the dish and bake for 25 to 30 minutes or until tender but not mushy. Place the apples on a lightly oiled baking pan and allow to cool thoroughly.
- When the apples have cooled, place one cup of sugar and a half cup cold water in a medium-size heavy saucepan over medium-high heat. Stir with a wooden spoon until the sugar has dissolved. When the sugar begins to turn golden, rotate the pan to even the color. When the caramel is light amber, using a wooden spoon, carefully coat each apple with the hot caramel. (Caramel burns quickly and must be watched carefully. It will continue to cook and become a darker amber as you are working with it.) Repeat the method with the remaining sugar, using a clean, cool, medium-size heavy saucepan.
- Meanwhile, whip the cream into soft peaks and fold in the ginger and refrigerate until ready to serve the apples.
- When ready to serve, pry the apples from the baking pans with a metal spatula and arrange them on a serving platter or serve on individual dessert plates, accompanied with the ginger cream.

Nutrition Information

- 405: calories;
- 5 grams: dietary fiber;
- 18 milligrams: sodium;
- 15 grams: fat;
- 0 grams: trans fat;
- 64 grams: sugars;
- 8 grams: saturated fat;
- 1 gram: protein;
- 71 grams: carbohydrates;

17. Caramelized Brown Butter Rice Krispies Treats

Serving: 30 to 50 treats | Prep: | Cook: | Ready in: 15mins

Ingredients

- 8 ounces butter, salted or unsalted, preferably cultured, plus extra for pan
- 2 10 1/2-ounce bag marshmallows (see note)
- 1 12-ounce box Rice Krispies cereal

Direction

- Line rimmed sheet pan with parchment paper or wax paper, or butter it well.
- In a large pot, melt butter over medium-low heat. It will melt, then foam, then turn clear golden and finally start to turn brown and smell nutty. Watch closely and stir often.
- When butter is evenly browned, stir in marshmallows. (If using unsalted butter, stir in 1/8 teaspoon salt.) Melt and cook, stirring often, until mixture turns pale brown, then stir constantly until lightly browned but not dark, 3 to 5 minutes.
- Turn off heat, add cereal, and mix well, preferably with a silicone spoon or a spatula. Scrape into prepared pan and press down lightly. If necessary, butter hands to press mixture flat. Let cool, and cut into squares or bars.

Nutrition Information

- 120: calories;
- 3 grams: saturated fat;
- 0 grams: dietary fiber;
- 1 gram: protein;
- 19 grams: carbohydrates;
- 9 grams: sugars;
- 57 milligrams: sodium;
- 5 grams: fat;

18. Caramelized Citrus

Serving: Serves 4-8 | Prep: | Cook: |Ready in: 30mins

Ingredients

- 4 assorted sweet citrus fruits, like blood or navel oranges or grapefruit
- 1 cup or 285 grams Greek-style yogurt
- 1 ½ cups or 300 grams light brown sugar
- 1 pinch saffron threads

Direction

- Using a small, sharp knife, cut off the tops and bottoms of the oranges and grapefruit, then slice the peel off them vertically, taking care to remove all the white pith below the skin of the fruit.
- Spoon the yogurt onto a platter or into a large bowl. Turn each fruit on its side, then slice it into rounds that are between 1/4-inch and 1/8-inch thick. Place the sliced fruit on top of the yogurt in an attractive pattern, then place the platter or bowl into the refrigerator.
- Make the caramel. Put the sugar in a large sauté pan set over medium heat, then add to it 1/2 cup or 125 milliliters of water, and swirl the pan to dissolve the sugar. Let the mixture come slowly to a boil, without stirring, then lower heat slightly, and cook until the syrup has gone a very deep amber color, approximately 5 to 6 minutes. Remove from heat, add the saffron to the caramel and swirl to mix it in.
- Pour the caramel over the sliced fruit. Return to the refrigerator for an hour or so, or serve right away.

Nutrition Information

- 53: calories;
- 0 grams: polyunsaturated fat;
- 13 grams: carbohydrates;
- 2 grams: dietary fiber;
- 12 grams: sugars;
- 1 gram: protein;
- 0 milligrams: sodium;

19. Caramelized Figs With Honey, Thyme And Crème Fraîche

Serving: 4 servings | Prep: | Cook: |Ready in: 15mins

Ingredients

- 3 tablespoons mild honey
- 6 plump figs, trimmed and halved

- 1 ½ tablespoons unsalted butter
- 4 fresh thyme sprigs, plus extra leaves for garnish
- 4 tablespoons crème fraîche

Direction

- Spoon the honey over the cut sides of the figs. Heat a large, heavy skillet over a medium-high flame. Add the butter — it should sizzle briskly when it hits the pan. Throw in the thyme sprigs, followed by the figs, cut sides down. Leave undisturbed for 3 to 5 minutes to caramelize, then turn the figs over and cook for another minute.
- Transfer the figs to a plate. Return the skillet to the heat and add about 5 tablespoons water. Simmer, scraping the caramelized honey with a spoon. Pour this sauce over the figs and serve warm with generous spoonfuls of crème fraîche and a few extra thyme leaves.

Nutrition Information

- 170: calories;
- 7 grams: fat;
- 0 grams: polyunsaturated fat;
- 26 grams: sugars;
- 9 milligrams: sodium;
- 4 grams: saturated fat;
- 2 grams: dietary fiber;
- 28 grams: carbohydrates;
- 1 gram: protein;

20. Caramelized Onion Dip With Frizzled Leeks

Serving: 8 servings | Prep: | Cook: | Ready in: 2hours

Ingredients

- 2 pounds onions (6 to 8 medium), chopped (5 to 6 cups)
- 6 tablespoons extra virgin olive oil, plus more as needed
- Salt
- freshly ground black pepper
- 1 tablespoon fresh thyme leaves
- 1 ½ cups whole-milk yogurt
- 1 tablespoon freshly squeezed lemon juice, or more to taste
- 2 leeks, trimmed, cleaned and julienned or thinly sliced
- Crudités or crackers for serving

Direction

- Put the onions in a large skillet over medium heat. Cover and cook, stirring infrequently, until the onions are dry and almost sticking to the pan, about 20 minutes. Stir in 2 tablespoons of the oil and a large pinch of salt and turn the heat down to medium-low. Cook, stirring occasionally and adding just enough additional oil to keep them from sticking without getting greasy. The onions are ready when they're dark, sweet and jammy, 40 minutes to 1 hour later.
- Sprinkle with black pepper, stir in the thyme and remove the onions from the heat. When they're cool, fold them into the yogurt and stir in the lemon juice. Taste and adjust the seasoning, then transfer the mixture to a serving bowl. (At this point, you can cover the dip with plastic wrap and refrigerate for up to 2 days.)
- Wipe or wash out the skillet and put it over medium-high heat. When it's hot, add the remaining 4 tablespoons oil. A few seconds later, add half the leeks, turn the heat up to high and sprinkle with salt and pepper. Use a spatula to turn the leeks over as they cook. Be careful: they will go from not-browned to burnt pretty quickly, and you want to catch them in between those stages, when they're browned and crisp. Transfer the leeks to paper towels to drain and repeat with the remaining leeks, adding more oil to the pan if necessary to keep them from sticking.

- Garnish the onion dip with the crisp leeks and serve immediately with crudités or crackers.

Nutrition Information

- 178: calories;
- 12 grams: fat;
- 2 grams: saturated fat;
- 8 grams: sugars;
- 1 gram: polyunsaturated fat;
- 16 grams: carbohydrates;
- 3 grams: protein;
- 445 milligrams: sodium;

21. Caramelized Onion And Lentil Pilaf

Serving: 6 servings | Prep: | Cook: | Ready in: 40mins

Ingredients

- 3 tablespoons ghee (clarified butter) or vegetable oil
- 1 onion, peeled, halved and thinly sliced into half-moons
- ½ teaspoon turmeric
- 1 teaspoon ground cumin
- 1 teaspoon ground coriander
- 2 cloves
- ½ teaspoon mustard seeds
- 4 dried curry leaves (optional)
- 2 teaspoons salt
- Black pepper
- 1 cup French green lentils
- 1 cup basmati rice

Direction

- In a large heavy-based saucepan, heat ghee over medium heat. Add onion slices, and sauté until softened and deep golden brown. Remove half the onions and set aside.
- Reduce heat to medium-low and add turmeric, cumin, coriander, cloves, mustard seeds and curry leaves. Add salt, and season with black pepper to taste.
- Combine lentils and rice in a fine-meshed sieve, and rinse well with cold water. Drain, then add to pan. Add 4 cups water, raise heat, and bring to a boil. Cover, reduce heat to very low, and cook for 15 to 20 minutes. Water should be completely absorbed; if not, remove pan from heat, remove lid and cover pan with a kitchen towel, then replace lid and allow to stand for 10 minutes.
- To serve, fluff pilaf with a fork, and transfer to a serving bowl. Garnish with reserved onions.

Nutrition Information

- 300: calories;
- 11 grams: protein;
- 214 milligrams: sodium;
- 8 grams: fat;
- 1 gram: polyunsaturated fat;
- 0 grams: trans fat;
- 48 grams: carbohydrates;
- 5 grams: dietary fiber;
- 2 grams: sugars;

22. Caramelized Onion And Mushroom Matzo Brei

Serving: 2 servings | Prep: | Cook: | Ready in: 20mins

Ingredients

- 3 tablespoons unsalted butter
- ⅓ cup diced onions
- ½ cup sliced mushrooms
- Salt and freshly ground black pepper, to taste
- 2 matzos (about 2 ounces), broken into pieces
- 5 large eggs, lightly beaten

Direction

- In a skillet over low heat, melt 2 tablespoons butter. Add onions and cook, stirring, until caramelized, 5 to 7 minutes.
- Add mushrooms and raise heat to medium-high. Continue to cook, stirring, until mushrooms are soft, about 5 minutes. Season with plenty of salt and pepper.
- Add remaining tablespoon butter to pan and let it melt. Add matzo and cook, tossing to coat matzo in butter, for 2 minutes.
- Pour eggs into pan and season them generously with salt and pepper. Cook, scrambling mixture, until eggs are set, about 2 to 3 more minutes. Season with salt and pepper and serve.

Nutrition Information

- 460: calories;
- 15 grams: saturated fat;
- 510 milligrams: sodium;
- 1 gram: trans fat;
- 9 grams: monounsaturated fat;
- 3 grams: polyunsaturated fat;
- 28 grams: carbohydrates;
- 2 grams: sugars;
- 20 grams: protein;
- 30 grams: fat;

23. Caramelized Peaches

Serving: 4 servings | Prep: | Cook: | Ready in: 20mins

Ingredients

- 1 29-ounce can peaches in heavy syrup (about 8 peach halves and 1 cup of syrup)
- ½ cup heavy cream
- 1 tablespoon Cognac
- 1 tablespoon fresh lemon juice
- 4 slices (1/2 inch thick) brioche or pound cake
- 2 tablespoons coarsely chopped pistachio nuts

Direction

- Drain peaches, pouring syrup into a skillet. Place skillet over high heat. Cook until syrup is caramelized (thick and light golden brown), about 10 minutes, stirring gently toward end of cooking so caramel does not burn around edges.
- Add peaches to caramel. Stir in cream. Bring to a boil, stirring occasionally. Boil 1 to 2 minutes. Transfer to bowl, and allow to cool.
- Stir in Cognac and lemon juice. If mixture is too thick, add 1 to 2 tablespoons water. Cover, and refrigerate until serving.
- To serve, toast brioche slices, and place one on each of four dessert plates. Arrange 2 peach halves on top of each slice, and top with a spoonful or two of sauce. Sprinkle with pistachios, and serve.

Nutrition Information

- 367: calories;
- 9 grams: saturated fat;
- 0 grams: trans fat;
- 4 grams: protein;
- 135 milligrams: sodium;
- 18 grams: fat;
- 6 grams: monounsaturated fat;
- 2 grams: polyunsaturated fat;
- 49 grams: carbohydrates;
- 39 grams: sugars;

24. Charlotte Aux Poires William Et Caramel

Serving: 8 servings | Prep: | Cook: | Ready in: 4hours25mins

Ingredients

- 5 egg yolks
- ¾ cup sugar
- 1 ½ cup milk
- 1 vanilla bean, split in half
- Pinch of salt

- 1 1/4-ounce package, plus 1 teaspoon, unflavored gelatin
- The caramel:
- ¼ cup sugar
- Pinch of salt
- ½ teaspoon vanilla extract
- 2 tablespoons water
- 2 cups creme chantilly
- 1 can (16 ounces) pears in syrup
- 12 to 16 ladyfingers, store-bought

Direction

- Place the egg yolks in a large bowl and add the sugar and pinch of salt. Beat the mixture until it is thick, with a light yellow color.
- Combine the milk and vanilla bean in a saucepan and bring the mixture almost, but not quite, to the boil.
- Remove the vanilla bean and gradually add the milk to the egg mixture, beating constantly until all the milk is fully incorporated. Pour this mixture back into a saucepan and cook over very low heat, constantly scraping the bottom with a spoon or whisk. Cook until it coats a spoon like a thick custard. Do not let the sauce boil, or it will curdle. Immediately remove the saucepan from the stove, stirring constantly.
- Dissolve the gelatin in a quarter cup of warm water and stir this into the warm sauce until it is thoroughly dissolved.
- While the custard is cooking, in a heavy pot or sugar pan, add the sugar, salt, vanilla extract and two tablespoons of water. Cook over medium-high heat without stirring, until it is richly browned but not burned. Add this caramel to the sauce. Allow the mixture to cool thoroughly.
- Make the whipped cream (see recipe). Fold the cream into the mixture. Drain very well the can of pears and cut them into half-inch pieces. Fold the pear pieces into the mixture.
- Line the bottom of a two-quart tinned charlotte mold with parchment paper. Cut and trim the ladyfingers into triangles. Arrange them tightly together in the bottom of the mold. Then arrange them on the sides of the mold by placing them parallel to each other.
- Fill the charlotte mold with the pear mixture to the top of the mold. Cover with plastic wrap and refrigerate. Let it rest for at least four hours in the refrigerator before unmolding.

Nutrition Information

- 271: calories;
- 5 grams: fat;
- 2 grams: monounsaturated fat;
- 1 gram: dietary fiber;
- 48 grams: carbohydrates;
- 34 grams: sugars;
- 9 grams: protein;
- 137 milligrams: sodium;

25. Chicken Livers With Caramelized Onions And Mushrooms

Serving: 4 servings | Prep: | Cook: |Ready in: 40mins

Ingredients

- 2 medium onions, cut in two and thinly sliced
- 2 tablespoons extra virgin olive oil or butter, more as needed
- Salt
- freshly ground black pepper
- 1 sprig fresh rosemary, finely chopped
- 1 cup button mushrooms, cleaned, trimmed and sliced
- 4 uncooked chicken livers (see note)
- 2 tablespoons sherry vinegar or other, or more to taste
- Crusty bread or toast for serving

Direction

- Put onions in a large skillet over medium heat. Cover and cook, stirring infrequently, until

onions are dry and almost sticking to pan, about 20 minutes.
- Stir in a tablespoon of oil or butter and a large pinch of salt and a few grindings of black pepper, add rosemary and turn heat down to medium-low. Add mushrooms and cook, stirring occasionally, until mushrooms release their liquid and it evaporates, about 15 minutes more. Remove vegetables from pan; set aside.
- Wipe pan with a paper towel, put it over medium-high heat and add remaining oil or butter. When oil is hot or foam from butter has subsided, add chicken livers. Keep heat high and cook livers quickly, turning them until brown and crisp on both sides but still pink on inside, about 3 or 4 minutes total. Remove from pan.
- Return vegetables to pan along with vinegar and 2 or 3 tablespoons water, just enough to deglaze; stir well to combine and serve with livers and crusty bread, or on toast.

Nutrition Information

- 142: calories;
- 7 grams: carbohydrates;
- 3 grams: sugars;
- 9 grams: protein;
- 2 grams: saturated fat;
- 0 grams: trans fat;
- 5 grams: monounsaturated fat;
- 1 gram: dietary fiber;
- 308 milligrams: sodium;

26. Clay Pot Pork

Serving: 4 servings | Prep: | Cook: |Ready in: 1hours15mins

Ingredients

- ⅓ cup sugar
- ¾ cup chicken stock, more if necessary
- 3 tablespoons fish sauce
- 3 shallots, thinly sliced
- 2 cloves garlic, thinly sliced
- 2 teaspoons minced ginger
- 1 teaspoon black pepper
- 1 small fresh chili, minced optional
- 3 scallions, trimmed and thinly sliced on the bias, green and white parts separated
- 1 ½ pound boneless pork shoulder or pork belly cut into 1-inch cubes
- Steamed white rice for serving

Direction

- Put the sugar in a medium-size heavy-bottomed pot and cook over medium heat, shaking gently every once in a while, until it starts to melt. Start stirring with a fork and continue, crushing clumps of sugar so that the sugar melts evenly. When the sugar is liquid, continue to cook for another minute or so until it darkens, then remove from heat.
- Combine the chicken stock and fish sauce and carefully add at arm's length to the sugar (it will splutter and pop). Turn heat to medium high, return sugar mixture to the heat, and cook, stirring constantly, until well combined. (If the sugar clumps when you add the liquid, don't worry, it will melt again.)
- Add the shallots, garlic, ginger, pepper, chili if using, and the white portion of the scallions. Cook, stirring frequently, until the shallots are nicely softened, 2 to 3 minutes.
- Add pork to the pot and bring the liquid to a boil. Reduce the heat to low, partly cover and simmer gently, stirring occasionally and adding a splash of stock or water if the pan looks too dry, until the pork is very tender and the liquid has reduced to a medium-thick sauce, about 1 hour.
- Remove from heat, add the green part of the scallions, and serve over steamed white rice.

Nutrition Information

- 527: calories;
- 31 grams: fat;

- 14 grams: monounsaturated fat;
- 3 grams: polyunsaturated fat;
- 28 grams: carbohydrates;
- 22 grams: sugars;
- 11 grams: saturated fat;
- 2 grams: dietary fiber;
- 33 grams: protein;
- 1243 milligrams: sodium;

27. Coconut Dulce De Leche With Caramelized Pineapple

Serving: 6 servings | Prep: | Cook: | Ready in: 30mins

Ingredients

- 2 (13 1/2-ounce) cans unsweetened coconut milk (not low-fat)
- 160 grams dark brown sugar (2/3 cup plus 2 tablespoons)
- 25 grams unsweetened coconut chips or flakes (1/2 cup)
- 1 small pineapple, peeled, cored and diced into 1/2-inch pieces (about 4 cups pineapple)
- Flaky sea salt, for garnish (optional)

Direction

- In a large skillet over low heat, combine coconut milk and 135 grams (2/3 cup) sugar. Cook gently, stirring and scraping down the sides of the pan occasionally, until mixture is a deep caramel color, smooth and spreadable, about 1 1/2 to 3 hours, depending on how powerful your stove is. The mixture should remain at a low simmer; do not let it come to a boil. Scrape into a bowl or container and let cool thoroughly, then chill for at least 2 hours and up to 5 days before serving.
- Heat oven to 325 degrees. Spread coconut on a rimmed baking sheet and toast until golden around the edges, 8 to 12 minutes. Let cool.
- Toss pineapple with remaining 25 grams (2 tablespoons) sugar. Let fruit stand until sugar dissolves, 1 to 2 minutes.
- Heat broiler and arrange an oven rack in the position closest to the flame. Spread fruit on a rimmed baking sheet. Broil 4 minutes. Stir, then broil until well-caramelized and charred in places, 3 to 4 minutes more.
- Spoon dulce de leche into 6 ramekins. Top each with warm pineapple and toasted coconut; sprinkle with salt if using and serve.

Nutrition Information

- 427: calories;
- 28 grams: saturated fat;
- 1 gram: monounsaturated fat;
- 0 grams: polyunsaturated fat;
- 3 grams: dietary fiber;
- 30 grams: sugars;
- 4 grams: protein;
- 32 grams: fat;
- 39 grams: carbohydrates;
- 26 milligrams: sodium;

28. Curried Spinach Stuffing With Caramelized Onions

Serving: Four servings | Prep: | Cook: | Ready in: 50mins

Ingredients

- ¾ cup plain lowfat yogurt
- 2 teaspoons olive oil
- 1 small onion, peeled and diced
- 2 teaspoons curry powder
- 6 cups coarsely chopped spinach
- 1 teaspoon salt
- Freshly ground pepper to taste
- 1 medium onion, peeled, halved lengthwise and thinly sliced

Direction

- Place the yogurt in a paper-towel-lined sieve and let stand until the liquid drips out, several hours or overnight.

- Heat 1 teaspoon of olive oil in a medium nonstick skillet over medium heat. Add the diced onion and cook until translucent, about 3 minutes. Lower the heat, stir in the curry powder and cook, stirring, for 3 minutes more. Add the spinach and saute for 3 to 4 minutes.
- Place the mixture in a blender and add the salt, pepper and yogurt. Blend until smooth. Place in a small saucepan and set aside.
- Heat the remaining oil in a medium-heavy skillet over medium heat. Add the sliced onion and cook, stirring often, until caramelized, about 30 minutes. Warm the spinach mixture. Fill the potatoes with the spinach stuffing and pile the caramelized onions on top. Serve.

Nutrition Information

- 81: calories;
- 10 grams: carbohydrates;
- 325 milligrams: sodium;
- 3 grams: fat;
- 0 grams: polyunsaturated fat;
- 4 grams: protein;
- 1 gram: saturated fat;
- 2 grams: dietary fiber;
- 5 grams: sugars;

29. Dried Fruit And Nut Bsteeyas

Serving: 4 servings | Prep: | Cook: | Ready in: 5hours

Ingredients

- For the fruit:
- ¼ cup dates in 1/8-inch dice
- ¼ cup apricots in 1/8-inch dice
- ¼ cup raisins
- ¼ cup brandy
- For the nuts:
- 2 tablespoons sugar
- 1 tablespoon unsalted butter
- 1 tablespoon each sliced almonds, whole pistachios, pine nuts, walnut halves
- 1 tablespoon of whole pistachios
- 1 tablespoon of pine nuts
- 1 tablespoons of walnut halves
- For the almond cream:
- 4 tablespoons unsalted butter, softened
- 4 ½ tablespoons sugar
- 1 egg yolk
- 4 ½ tablespoons almond flour
- ½ teaspoon ground cinnamon
- ½ teaspoon ground ginger
- 6 sheets phyllo dough
- 4 tablespoons unsalted butter, melt
- For serving:
- Confectioners' sugar
- Ground cinnamon
- Ginger ice cream

Direction

- For the fruit: mix all ingredients in 1/4 cup of warm water and leave to macerate and rehydrate for at least four hours.
- For the nuts: lightly grease a baking sheet and set aside. In a skillet, melt sugar over medium heat and cook, swirling the pan, until it reaches a dark caramel color. Add butter, then nuts, and stir until nuts are covered with caramel and butter, about 5 minutes. Spread mixture on baking sheet to cool.
- For the almond cream: beat butter and sugar together in a bowl until smooth, add egg yolk, mix well, then stir in flour, cinnamon and ginger.
- Preheat oven to 375 degrees. Line a baking sheet with parchment and set aside.
- Cut phyllo sheets in half and work with three pieces at a time, keeping the remaining sheets covered with plastic wrap so they don't dry out. Brush one piece with melted butter, place another half sheet on top at a 45-degree angle and brush with more butter. Place third in opposite direction at a 45-degree angle and brush with butter. Carefully lifting sheets, slide a 4-inch saucer under phyllo. Spread 1/8 of almond cream in phyllo center, sprinkle almond cream with 1/4 of nuts and 1/4 of fruit, then cover with another 1/8 of cream.

Fold phyllo flaps over center, creating a disk-shaped pie. Brush with butter. Repeat to make three more bsteeyas. Place on baking sheet.
- Bake until golden brown, about 15 minutes, turning over after 7 minutes. Remove from oven. Dust with a little sugar and cinnamon. Serve with ginger ice cream.

Nutrition Information

- 622: calories;
- 38 grams: fat;
- 10 grams: monounsaturated fat;
- 7 grams: protein;
- 145 milligrams: sodium;
- 18 grams: saturated fat;
- 1 gram: trans fat;
- 4 grams: dietary fiber;
- 61 grams: carbohydrates;
- 39 grams: sugars;

30. Duck Or Rabbit Livers With Onion Marmalade

Serving: Serves 6 | Prep: | Cook: | Ready in: 1hours30mins

Ingredients

- 8 tablespoons butter
- 1 ½ pounds onions, peeled and thinly sliced
- ½ cup sugar
- 1½ teaspoons salt
- 7 tablespoons sherry vinegar
- 1 cup inexpensive red wine
- 1 pound duck or rabbit livers
- 1 teaspoon pepper
- 2 tablespoons cooking oil

Direction

- First, make the marmalade. Sizzle the butter in a saucepan over medium-high heat until it is nut brown, 3 to 4 minutes, then immediately add the onions, sugar and ½ teaspoon of the salt. Reduce the heat and stew gently until the onions are dark caramel brown, 30 to 45 minutes, being careful to not blacken them. Add the vinegar and wine and cook for another 30 minutes, stirring from time to time, until the butter floats separately from the onions. You need only a few spoonfuls of this for the livers, but don't be angry! The ingredients were cheap, and this will keep for weeks, stored in a jar in the refrigerator. From thence it shall come to enliven sandwiches, charcuterie, roasts and all kinds of other stuff.
- On to the livers. Warm a plate in a low oven. Trim, rinse and pat the livers dry; season with the pepper and the remaining salt. Warm the oil in a nonstick skillet and fry the livers for about a minute and a half per side. Let them rest for 5 minutes on the warm plate, then slice and serve with a few tablespoons of marmalade on polenta, toast or crêpes parmentier (see recipe here).

Nutrition Information

- 425: calories;
- 1 gram: trans fat;
- 7 grams: monounsaturated fat;
- 2 grams: dietary fiber;
- 17 grams: protein;
- 23 grams: fat;
- 11 grams: saturated fat;
- 32 grams: carbohydrates;
- 22 grams: sugars;
- 642 milligrams: sodium;

31. Endive Cheese Tart

Serving: 6 to 8 servings | Prep: | Cook: | Ready in: 2hours45mins

Ingredients

- For the dough

- ½ cup confectioners' sugar
- 1 cup all-purpose flour
- Pinch of salt
- 4 ½ tablespoons unsalted butter, at room temperature, cut into small pieces
- 1 large egg
- For the filling
- 3 pounds small Belgian endives, trimmed of brown edges
- 8 tablespoons unsalted butter
- ½ cup granulated sugar
- ½ pound Époisses cheese

Direction

-
-

Nutrition Information

- 446: calories;
- 6 grams: dietary fiber;
- 20 grams: sugars;
- 11 grams: protein;
- 7 grams: monounsaturated fat;
- 1 gram: polyunsaturated fat;
- 39 grams: carbohydrates;
- 234 milligrams: sodium;
- 29 grams: fat;
- 17 grams: saturated fat;

32. English Pea And Onion Salad

Serving: 6 servings | Prep: | Cook: | Ready in: 30mins

Ingredients

- 5 ounces slab bacon, cut into 1/4-inch cubes
- 2 lemons, zested and juiced
- 1 tablespoon extra-virgin olive oil
- 1 small onion, diced and rinsed under cold water
- 3 tablespoons mayonnaise
- 4 tablespoons grated Parmesan cheese
- 4 tablespoons mixed chopped fresh herbs, such as parsley, mint, tarragon and basil
- 2 large eggs, hard-cooked and finely diced
- Salt and pepper
- 2 cups fresh or thawed frozen peas
- 2 tablespoons sliced almonds, toasted
- 2 tablespoons bread crumbs, toasted

Direction

- Heat oven to 400 degrees and line a baking sheet with foil. Spread bacon cubes on baking sheet and cook until caramelized and crispy, 15 to 20 minutes. Strain off rendered fat and set aside to cool.
- Meanwhile, combine lemon zest and juice, olive oil, onion, mayonnaise, 2 tablespoons Parmesan, 2 tablespoons fresh herbs and the eggs in a large bowl. Season with salt and pepper to taste.
- If you're using fresh peas, chop them to tenderize; if using frozen, strain off excess moisture. Fold peas into dressing. Transfer mixture to a shallow serving bowl and spread in an even layer.
- Sprinkle remaining 2 tablespoons fresh herbs over the top, then create a layer of the remaining 2 tablespoons Parmesan cheese. Top with almonds, then bread crumbs and finally bacon.

Nutrition Information

- 301: calories;
- 6 grams: polyunsaturated fat;
- 13 grams: carbohydrates;
- 4 grams: sugars;
- 23 grams: fat;
- 7 grams: saturated fat;
- 0 grams: trans fat;
- 9 grams: monounsaturated fat;
- 3 grams: dietary fiber;
- 12 grams: protein;
- 419 milligrams: sodium;

33. Florence Fabricant's Praline

Serving: 2 cups | Prep: | Cook: |Ready in: 20mins

Ingredients

- 2 cups chopped almonds, hazelnuts or pecans
- 2 cups sugar
- ¼ cup water
- A large potato, peeled and cut in half

Direction

- Oil a large foil-covered baking sheet, marble slab or similar smooth surface.
- Lightly toast the nuts under the broiler, in a toaster oven or in a heavy, ungreased skillet on top of the stove. Watch carefully so they do not become too dark. Set aside.
- Combine the sugar and water in a wide, heavy saucepan or skillet and cook over medium-high heat, stirring occasionally until the mixture turns gold, then stir in the nuts and continue cooking until the mixture becomes honey brown.
- Pour the mixture out onto the prepared work surface and using the cut side of the potato, spread it thinly and evenly on the surface. Allow to cool completely.
- When the praline has cooled it can be broken into pieces to use as candy. The pieces can be stored in an airtight container in a dry cupboard. Some or all the praline can be chopped or ground coarsely or finely to use as a dessert topping or as an ingredient in desserts such as ice cream or cake. It should also be kept in an airtight container in a dry cupboard.

Nutrition Information

- 291: calories;
- 3 milligrams: sodium;
- 12 grams: fat;
- 1 gram: saturated fat;
- 8 grams: monounsaturated fat;
- 3 grams: polyunsaturated fat;
- 35 grams: sugars;
- 0 grams: trans fat;
- 44 grams: carbohydrates;
- 4 grams: dietary fiber;
- 6 grams: protein;

34. Foolproof Tarte Tatin

Serving: 8 servings | Prep: | Cook: |Ready in: 1hours30mins

Ingredients

- 6 to 8 large, firm-fleshed apples, preferably Braeburn, or use a mix of Honeycrisp and Granny Smith
- 6 tablespoons/80 grams salted butter, very soft
- ⅔ cup/135 grams granulated or light brown sugar
- 1 sheet all-butter puff pastry, about 8 ounces (store-bought is fine)

Direction

- At least one day before you plan to cook the tart, prepare the apples: Slice off the bottom of each apple so it has a flat base. Peel and quarter the apples. Use a small sharp knife to trim the hard cores and seeds from the center of each quarter, don't worry about being too neat. Transfer to a bowl and refrigerate, lightly covered, for at least one day or up to three days. (This key step reduces the amount of liquid in the tart. Don't worry if the apples turn brown; they will be browned during the cooking anyway.)
- When ready to cook, heat oven to 375 degrees (or 350 if using convection). Thickly coat the bottom of a 10-inch heavy ovenproof skillet, preferably nonstick metal, with butter. Sprinkle sugar evenly on top.
- Cut one piece of apple into a thick round disk and place in the center of the skillet to serve as the "button." Arrange the remaining apple

pieces, each one standing on its flat end, in concentric circles around the button. Keep the pieces close together so that they support one another, standing upright. They will look like the petals of a flower.
- On a floured surface, roll out the puff pastry about 1/8-inch thick. Place an upside-down bowl or pan on the pastry and use the tip of a sharp knife to cut out a circle about the same size as the top of your skillet. Lift out the circle and drape gently over the apples. Use your hands to tuck the pastry around the apple pieces, hugging them together firmly.
- Place the skillet on the stovetop over medium heat until golden-brown juice begins to bubble around the edges, 3 minutes (if the juices keep rising, spoon out as needed to remain level with pastry). If necessary, raise the heat so that the juices are at a boil. Keep cooking until the juices are turning darker brown and smell caramelized, no longer than 10 minutes more.
- Transfer skillet to the oven and bake 45 to 50 minutes, until puff pastry is browned and firm.
- Let cool 5 minutes, then carefully turn out onto a round serving plate. (Or, if not serving immediately, let cool completely in the pan; when ready to serve, rewarm for 15 minutes in a 350-degree oven before turning out.) If any apples remain stuck in the pan, gently use your fingers or a spatula to retrieve them, and rearrange on the pastry shell. Cut in wedges and serve warm with heavy cream, crème fraîche or vanilla ice cream.

Nutrition Information

- 242: calories;
- 1 gram: protein;
- 78 milligrams: sodium;
- 10 grams: fat;
- 5 grams: saturated fat;
- 39 grams: carbohydrates;
- 31 grams: sugars;
- 0 grams: polyunsaturated fat;
- 3 grams: monounsaturated fat;
- 4 grams: dietary fiber;

35. Glazed Mango With Sour Cream Sorbet And Black Pepper

Serving: 4 servings | Prep: | Cook: | Ready in: 30mins

Ingredients

- 2 large mangoes, ripe but not soft
- 4 tablespoons unsalted butter, plus butter for baking sheet
- ⅓ cup sugar
- ⅓ cup lemon juice
- Freshly ground black pepper
- 1 cup passion fruit sauce (see recipe)
- Sour cream sorbet (see recipe)
- 1 teaspoon coarse black pepper

Direction

- Peel mangoes. Cut in thirds horizontally, leaving the pit in middle section. Place each portion without pit cut-side down on a work surface, and with a large knife cut into 8 slices perpendicular to the cutting board. Gently push down on slices so they spread out and overlap slightly.
- Sliver enough mango flesh left around the pits to make 1/2 cup. Set slivers aside.
- Butter a baking sheet large enough to hold mangoes in a single layer. Heat the broiler.
- Melt remaining butter in a large nonstick skillet. Use a spatula to place each sliced mango third in the pan so they keep their shape. Cook over medium heat about 5 minutes, sprinkling with two tablespoons sugar, and basting with pan juices.
- With spatula, transfer mangoes to baking sheet, place under broiler, and broil until edges just start to color. Do not overcook. Set mangoes aside.
- Add remaining sugar to juices in skillet, and cook over medium heat until juices start to caramelize. Add lemon juice, and continue to

cook, stirring, until amber colored. Season lightly with pepper. Spoon on mangoes.
- Place a sliced caramelized mango third in each of 4 shallow soup plates. Spoon passion fruit sauce around each, and scatter raw mango slivers around. Top each with a large oval scoop of sour cream sorbet, sprinkle 1/4 teaspoon coarse pepper on top and serve at once.

36. Grilled Peach Sundaes With Salted Bourbon Caramel Sauce

Serving: Serves 4 | Prep: | Cook: | Ready in: 1hours

Ingredients

- For the peaches:
- 4 ripe peaches
- 3 tablespoons peanut oil
- Sea salt
- For the pecans:
- 1 cup whole pecan halves
- 1 ½ tablespoons melted butter
- ¾ teaspoon salt
- ¼ teaspoon cayenne
- 1 ½ tablespoons sugar
- For the caramel:
- 1 cup sugar
- ¼ cup water
- 2 tablespoons light corn syrup
- ¾ cup heavy cream
- 4 tablespoons butter
- 1 teaspoon sea salt
- ¼ cup bourbon
- For the whipped cream:
- 1 cup best-quality heavy cream
- 3 tablespoons powdered sugar
- 1 teaspoon vanilla
- ¼ cup buttermilk

Direction

-

Nutrition Information

- 1130: calories;
- 1 gram: trans fat;
- 5 grams: dietary fiber;
- 6 grams: protein;
- 997 milligrams: sodium;
- 91 grams: carbohydrates;
- 87 grams: sugars;
- 83 grams: fat;
- 37 grams: saturated fat;
- 30 grams: monounsaturated fat;
- 11 grams: polyunsaturated fat;

37. Hete Bliksem

Serving: 4 servings | Prep: | Cook: | Ready in: 1hours30mins

Ingredients

- For the syrup
- ¾ cup sugar
- 2 tablespoons unsalted butter
- ½ cup heavy cream
- 1 tablespoon unsulfured molasses
- ¼ teaspoon kosher salt
- ½ teaspoon juniper berries, whole
- ½ nutmeg, cracked, or a pinch of freshly ground nutmeg
- ½ blade of mace, or a pinch of ground mace
- 1 cinnamon stick, broken in half
- For the potatoes
- 1 pound fingerling potatoes
- Kosher salt
- 1 head garlic, halved crosswise
- 4 sprigs thyme
- 4 bay leaves
- ½ teaspoon cayenne pepper
- For the rest
- 8 ounces sliced bacon, cut crosswise into 1/2-inch thick lardons

- Vegetable oil, for frying
- ½ cup rice flour, or as needed
- 1 large Honeycrisp apple, cored, seeded and cut into small dice
- Salt
- Cayenne pepper

Direction

- For the syrup: In a small saucepan, heat the sugar without stirring until it begins to melt. Stir occasionally until completely melted and a medium caramel color. Carefully stir in butter, cream and molasses. Add salt, juniper berries, nutmeg, mace and cinnamon. Stir until smooth. Remove from heat and steep for 30 minutes, then strain through a fine-meshed strainer. While the syrup is steeping, prepare the poached potatoes.
- For the potatoes: Place the potatoes in a medium saucepan and cover with two inches of water and season heavily with salt. Add garlic, thyme, bay leaves and cayenne pepper. On low heat, poach the potatoes until tender but not bursting, about 25 minutes. Gently strain potatoes and discard garlic, thyme and bay leaves. Set potatoes aside until no longer steaming, then transfer to the refrigerator to cool.
- For the rest: In a large skillet over medium heat, spread out the bacon and cook, stirring occasionally, until crisp and golden brown. Transfer to paper towels to drain and cool.
- In a wok or deep skillet, pour in vegetable oil to fry the potatoes, heat to 350 degrees. Cut the potatoes into 1-inch slices, and dust thoroughly with rice flour. Shake off excess flour, and place potatoes in the oil. Fry until golden brown and crispy, 2 to 3 minutes. Transfer to paper towels to drain.
- In a serving bowl, combine the syrup, bacon and apples. Add the potatoes and toss gently to mix. Season to taste with salt and cayenne. Serve.

Nutrition Information

- 1217: calories;
- 13 grams: protein;
- 92 grams: carbohydrates;
- 6 grams: dietary fiber;
- 915 milligrams: sodium;
- 1 gram: trans fat;
- 91 grams: fat;
- 22 grams: saturated fat;
- 51 grams: monounsaturated fat;
- 49 grams: sugars;

38. Honey Apple Pie With Thyme

Serving: One 9-inch single pie, 8 servings | Prep: | Cook: | Ready in: 1hours45mins

Ingredients

- 3 Golden Delicious apples, peeled and cored (about 1 1/4 pounds)
- 4 Granny Smith apples, peeled and cored (about 1 1/2 pounds)
- ½ cup honey
- 6 thyme branches
- ¼ cup unsalted butter (1/2 stick), cut into small pieces
- 2 tablespoons instant tapioca
- ⅓ cup light brown sugar
- ½ teaspoon ground ginger
- ¼ teaspoon salt
- Flour, for dusting
- Dough for 2 9-inch pie crusts (see recipe)

Direction

- Preheat oven to 425 degrees. Slice Golden Delicious apples and 3 Granny Smith apples into sixths.
- In a large skillet over medium-high heat, bring 1/4 cup honey to a boil. Let simmer about 2 minutes, until honey is caramelized. Add 3 thyme branches. Arrange half the apples in a single layer in skillet. Sprinkle 2 tablespoons butter over apples. Cook apples, turning, until well caramelized on all sides (but not cooked

through), about 10 minutes. Scrape apples and honey mixture into a bowl. Add tapioca and toss to combine. Repeat cooking process with remaining honey, thyme, butter and sliced apples. Add second batch of apples to bowl; combine. Discard all thyme branches.
- Thinly slice remaining Granny Smith apple and add it to bowl. Stir in sugar, ginger and salt.
- On a lightly floured surface, roll out both crusts to 12-inch circles. Place one crust in 9-inch pie plate. Scrape apple filling into crust and top with remaining crust. Pinch edges to seal. With a knife, slice 4 vents in top of crust. Place pie on a foil-lined, rimmed baking sheet.
- Bake for 15 minutes; reduce heat to 350 degrees and continue baking until crust is dark golden and apples are tender when pricked with a fork, about 45 minutes more. Let cool for 30 minutes before slicing.

Nutrition Information

- 384: calories;
- 8 grams: fat;
- 2 grams: monounsaturated fat;
- 74 grams: carbohydrates;
- 6 grams: protein;
- 0 grams: trans fat;
- 1 gram: polyunsaturated fat;
- 37 grams: sugars;
- 428 milligrams: sodium;
- 4 grams: saturated fat;

39. Irish Cream Caramel Sauce

Serving: 0 3/4 cup | Prep: | Cook: | Ready in: 15mins

Ingredients

- ½ cup sugar
- 4 tablespoons water
- ½ cup heavy cream
- 3 tablespoons Irish whisky (see note)

Direction

- Swirl sugar and water together in a heavy saucepan until the sugar dissolves. Place over medium-high heat and cook, stirring occasionally, until the mixture turns a uniform honey-brown color. Remove from heat.
- Pour a tablespoon or two of the cream into the caramel, standing back from the pan, because the mixture may spatter. Stir to blend in the cream, then add the remaining cream, stirring until completely mixed.
- Stir in the whisky, transfer the mixture to a jar or other container and refrigerate until ready to use. The sauce may be warmed before using but it will not be as thick as if it is chilled. Serve over ice cream, crepes, cake or puddings.

Nutrition Information

- 601: calories;
- 1 gram: polyunsaturated fat;
- 69 grams: sugars;
- 2 grams: protein;
- 33 milligrams: sodium;
- 29 grams: fat;
- 18 grams: saturated fat;
- 8 grams: monounsaturated fat;

40. Irish Oatmeal Brulee With Dried Fruit And Maple Cream

Serving: 4 servings | Prep: | Cook: | Ready in: 30mins

Ingredients

- 1 cup steel-cut oats
- 1 cup heavy cream
- 2 star anise
- 1 small cinnamon stick
- 1 small strip (1/2 by 1 1/2 inches) orange zest
- ¼ cup maple syrup
- Pinch of salt

- ¼ cup chopped dried apricots
- ¼ cup dried cherries or cranberries
- ¼ cup chopped dried figs
- 2 tablespoons toasted chopped pecans
- 2 tablespoons toasted chopped walnuts
- 4 tablespoons sugar

Direction

- Place oats in a bowl, and cover with water by 2 inches. Cover bowl, and let stand overnight.
- In a small saucepan, combine cream, star anise, cinnamon stick and orange zest. Bring mixture to a simmer, and cook for 10 minutes. Using a slotted spoon, remove spices and orange. Whisk maple syrup into cream, increase heat to medium-high and simmer until mixture thickens enough to coat back of a spoon, about 10 minutes.
- Meanwhile, drain oats and place them in a saucepan with 3 1/4 cups water. Simmer over medium heat until tender but not mushy, about 15 minutes. Stir in salt.
- Preheat broiler. In a small bowl, combine dried fruit and nuts. Divide half the oatmeal among four broiler-proof bowls or large ramekins, then top with fruits and nuts. Cover with remaining oatmeal, and smooth tops. Sprinkle 1 tablespoon sugar over each, and place under broiler. Broil until sugar caramelizes and forms a crust, about 1 to 2 minutes. Watch carefully so sugar doesn't burn. Serve immediately with maple cream.

Nutrition Information

- 505: calories;
- 28 grams: fat;
- 14 grams: saturated fat;
- 42 grams: sugars;
- 6 grams: protein;
- 101 milligrams: sodium;
- 8 grams: monounsaturated fat;
- 4 grams: polyunsaturated fat;
- 62 grams: carbohydrates;
- 5 grams: dietary fiber;

41. Linguine With Crab Meat

Serving: 4 servings | Prep: | Cook: | Ready in: 30mins

Ingredients

- 1 jalapeño, cored, seeded, very finely minced
- Zest of 1 lemon
- 1 tablespoon yuzu juice (sold in Japanese markets) or lemon juice
- 4 tablespoons extra virgin olive oil
- 1 medium onion, sliced
- 4 ounces button mushrooms, sliced
- ½ cup chopped peeled and seeded tomato, fresh or canned
- Salt
- Japanese togarashi pepper or cayenne, to taste
- 2 cloves garlic, thinly sliced
- 1 cup dry white wine
- 1 cup seafood stock
- ½ pound crab meat, preferably peekytoe
- 12 ounces fresh linguine
- 3 tablespoons unsalted butter
- 1 tablespoon chopped tarragon leaves

Direction

- Combine jalapeño, lemon zest and yuzu juice in a small dish and set aside. Heat half the oil in a large sauté pan. Add the onion and cook on medium-high until it starts to caramelize. Remove it. Add the mushrooms to the pan and cook until they start to brown. Return the onions to the pan, add the tomatoes and cook until they start to dry out. Pulse the mixture in a food processor until very finely chopped. Add the jalapeño mixture and season to taste with salt and togarashi. The mixture should have a touch of heat.
- Bring a pot of salted water to a boil for the pasta. Heat the remaining oil in the sauté pan on low. Add the garlic, cook until it softens, then add the wine. Increase heat to medium high and reduce until the wine films the pan. Add the stock and the tomato mixture. Stir, then add the crab.

- Cook the pasta until it is al dente, about 3 minutes. Drain and add it to the sauté pan. Add the butter. Use tongs to toss all the ingredients together. Divide among 4 warm plates, scatter tarragon on each and serve.

Nutrition Information

- 586: calories;
- 0 grams: trans fat;
- 3 grams: polyunsaturated fat;
- 2 grams: dietary fiber;
- 23 grams: protein;
- 25 grams: fat;
- 8 grams: saturated fat;
- 884 milligrams: sodium;
- 13 grams: monounsaturated fat;
- 57 grams: carbohydrates;
- 4 grams: sugars;

42. Maple Sugar Creme Caramel

Serving: 6 servings | Prep: | Cook: | Ready in: 1hours

Ingredients

- For the maple-sugar caramel:
- 1 cup maple sugar
- 1 tablespoon unsalted butter
- For the maple-sugar custard:
- 4 whole eggs
- 2 egg yolks
- 2 ½ cups milk
- 1 cup maple sugar

Direction

- Set out 6 6-ounce custard cups or ramekins. Combine 1/2 cup water and 1 cup maple sugar in a small saucepan. Bring to a boil over medium-high heat. Reduce heat to medium, and simmer for 5 minutes or until the syrup looks dark and shiny and is thick enough to coat a spoon. Remove from the heat, and whip in the butter. Spoon evenly into the bottom of each cup. Allow to cool; the syrup will thicken.
- Preheat oven to 325 degrees. Bring about 1 quart water to a boil for the water bath (bain-marie). Combine the eggs, egg yolks, milk and maple sugar. Mix very well, so that the sugar dissolves completely.
- Spoon about 2/3 cup of custard into each cup. Place the cups in a baking pan, and fill with enough boiling water to come about halfway up the sides of the cups. Cover loosely with aluminum foil and bake for about 35 minutes, or until set. A toothpick inserted into the center should come out clean.
- Chill thoroughly for about 2 hours. Loosen the custards with a small knife, and unmold onto plates. Be sure to serve all the sauce from each cup. Top with sweetened whipped cream, if desired.

Nutrition Information

- 304: calories;
- 49 grams: carbohydrates;
- 92 milligrams: sodium;
- 9 grams: fat;
- 0 grams: trans fat;
- 1 gram: polyunsaturated fat;
- 4 grams: saturated fat;
- 3 grams: monounsaturated fat;
- 46 grams: sugars;
- 8 grams: protein;

43. Matzo Brei With Caramelized Apples

Serving: 6 servings | Prep: | Cook: | Ready in: 30mins

Ingredients

- ½ cup honey
- 1 vanilla bean
- 9 tablespoons unsalted butter

- 2 Granny Smith apples, peeled, cored and cut into 1/2-inch cubes
- 2 tablespoons sugar
- 1 1-pound box matzo
- 8 large eggs
- 1 teaspoon kosher salt
- 4 ounces mascarpone cheese (or yogurt)

Direction

- Place honey in a small saucepan or microwavable bowl. Split vanilla bean lengthwise and use tip of knife to scrape seeds into honey. Add bean to honey as well. Gently warm honey over low heat or in microwave until it thins enough to easily pour, about 1 to 2 minutes. Keep warm or reheat before serving.
- Heat a sauté pan until very hot. Add 2 tablespoons butter, the apples and sugar. Fry, stirring occasionally, until apples are soft and caramelized, 8 to 10 minutes. Transfer to a dish and keep warm.
- Place matzos in a large bowl and cover with warm water. Soak for 1 minute, then drain, pressing to remove excess water.
- In a large bowl, lightly beat eggs with salt. Break soaked matzo into large pieces, adding them to eggs, and toss well.
- Melt 6 tablespoons butter in a 10-inch nonstick pan over medium-low heat. Add matzo and eggs and cook, pressing down on top with a spatula, until crisp on bottom, about 8 minutes. Use a flexible metal spatula to loosen bottom and sides, then invert pan over a plate to flip matzo brei. Add remaining tablespoon butter to pan and swirl to coat bottom. Slide matzo brei back into pan and continue to cook until a crust has formed on bottom and it is cooked through, about 3 to 5 more minutes.
- Cut matzo brei into 6 pieces. Top each piece with apples and a spoonful of mascarpone, and serve drizzled with honey vanilla sauce.

Nutrition Information

- 750: calories;
- 4 grams: dietary fiber;
- 18 grams: protein;
- 31 grams: fat;
- 17 grams: saturated fat;
- 100 grams: carbohydrates;
- 481 milligrams: sodium;
- 1 gram: trans fat;
- 9 grams: monounsaturated fat;
- 3 grams: polyunsaturated fat;
- 34 grams: sugars;

44. Pasta With Caramelized Onion, Swiss Chard And Garlicky Bread Crumbs

Serving: 2 to 3 servings | Prep: | Cook: | Ready in: 40mins

Ingredients

- 3 tablespoons butter or olive oil
- 5 anchovy fillets
- 2 garlic cloves, finely chopped
- ⅔ cup bread crumbs
- 1 tablespoon extra virgin olive oil, plus additional for drizzling
- 1 yellow onion, halved from stem to root and thinly sliced crosswise
- Kosher salt
- pepper
- 1 pound Swiss chard, ribs removed, leaves chopped
- ½ pound whole-wheat pasta, such as fusilli

Direction

- In a large skillet over medium heat, melt the butter. Add 3 anchovies to the skillet; cook until melted, about 2 minutes. Add the garlic and cook 1 minute. Stir in the bread crumbs and toast until golden, 3 to 4 minutes. Transfer to a bowl.
- Wipe the skillet clean and return it to a medium-high heat. Add the oil, the onion and

a pinch of salt. Cook, stirring occasionally, until very soft and caramelized, 15 to 20 minutes. Chop the remaining 2 anchovies and add them to the skillet. Cook until melted. Add the Swiss chard, a handful at a time, and cook until wilted, about 4 minutes. Cover and keep warm.
- Bring a large pot of salted water to a boil. Add the pasta and cook according to package directions. Drain well. Toss with the chard mixture and bread crumbs, season with salt and pepper and drizzle with oil.

Nutrition Information

- 559: calories;
- 18 grams: protein;
- 749 milligrams: sodium;
- 17 grams: fat;
- 3 grams: polyunsaturated fat;
- 11 grams: monounsaturated fat;
- 85 grams: carbohydrates;
- 7 grams: sugars;

45. Pasta With Fried Lemons And Chile Flakes

Serving: 4 to 6 servings | Prep: | Cook: | Ready in: 30mins

Ingredients

- 4 lemons
- 1 pound linguine or spaghetti
- 4 tablespoons extra-virgin olive oil, more for drizzling
- 1 teaspoon kosher salt, more as needed
- Pinch of sugar
- 3 tablespoons unsalted butter
- ¾ teaspoon chile flakes, more to taste
- ⅔ cup Parmigiano-Reggiano cheese, more to taste
- Black pepper, as needed
- ½ cup celery leaves, coarsely chopped (optional)
- ⅓ cup parsley, coarsely chopped (optional)
- Flaky sea salt, for garnish

Direction

- Bring a large pot of salted water to a boil. Finely zest 2 of the lemons and set aside. Trim the tops and bottoms off the other 2 lemons and cut lengthwise into quarters; remove seeds. Thinly slice the quarters crosswise into triangles. Blanch the lemon pieces in the boiling water for 2 minutes, then transfer with a slotted spoon to a dish towel. Blot dry.
- In the boiling water, add pasta and cook until just barely al dente. Drain, reserving 1/2 cup of the pasta cooking water.
- Meanwhile, in a large skillet, heat 1 tablespoon of the oil over high heat. Add the dried lemon pieces and season with a pinch each of salt and sugar. Cook until the lemons are caramelized and browned at the edges, 3 to 5 minutes. Transfer to a plate.
- Melt the butter with the remaining oil in the pan over medium heat. Add the chile flakes and zest of both lemons; cook until fragrant. Whisk in the reserved pasta water.
- Toss in pasta, juice of 1 lemon, cheese, pepper and the remaining salt. Cook until pasta is well coated with sauce. Toss in the caramelized lemon and the celery leaves and parsley if using. Taste and add lemon juice if needed. Serve, topped with a drizzle of oil, more cheese if you like, and a sprinkle of sea salt.

Nutrition Information

- 394: calories;
- 6 grams: saturated fat;
- 0 grams: trans fat;
- 1 gram: polyunsaturated fat;
- 15 grams: protein;
- 10 grams: fat;
- 3 grams: sugars;
- 61 grams: carbohydrates;

- 4 grams: dietary fiber;
- 313 milligrams: sodium;

46. Peach Upside Down Skillet Cake With Bourbon Whipped Cream

Serving: 8 servings | Prep: | Cook: |Ready in: 1hours15mins

Ingredients

- For the cake:
- 4 medium peaches (about 1 1/2 pounds/680 grams), unpeeled and cut into 1/3-inch-thick wedges
- Juice of 1 lemon
- 1 cup/130 grams cake flour, not self-rising
- ¾ teaspoon baking powder
- ¼ teaspoon baking soda
- 1 cup/200 grams granulated sugar
- 5 ounces/140 grams unsalted butter (1 stick plus 2 tablespoons), at cool room temperature
- 1 vanilla bean, split and seeds scraped, or 1 teaspoon pure vanilla extract
- 2 large eggs
- ½ cup sour cream
- For the bourbon whipped cream (optional):
- ½ cup heavy cream
- 1 tablespoon bourbon

Direction

- Heat oven to 350 degrees. Line a rimmed baking sheet with a nonstick baking mat or parchment paper. (This is in case the cake bubbles over during baking.)
- In a large bowl, toss the peaches with the lemon juice. In a separate bowl, whisk together the flour, baking powder and baking soda.
- In a 10-inch cast-iron skillet, cook 1/4 cup of the granulated sugar over medium heat, stirring occasionally with a wooden spoon, until the sugar melts and turns a deep amber color, about 10 minutes. Remove from the heat and immediately add 2 tablespoons of the butter, stirring vigorously. The mixture may appear curdled and broken; don't worry, it will smooth out. Arrange the peach wedges in concentric circles over the sugar mixture, overlapping as needed to make them fit.
- In a stand mixer fitted with the paddle attachment, beat the remaining sugar, butter and the vanilla bean seeds (or vanilla extract) on medium speed until smooth. Add the eggs one at a time, beating until blended after each addition. Add the sour cream and beat until blended. With the mixer running on low speed, gradually add the flour mixture, beating just until blended and stopping to scrape bowl as needed. Spoon the batter over the peaches in the skillet and spread to cover.
- Place the skillet on the prepared baking sheet. Bake until golden brown and a tester inserted into the center of the cake comes out clean, 40 to 45 minutes.
- Make the whipped cream, if desired: In a large bowl, preferably metal, combine cream and bourbon. Refrigerate, along with a metal whisk or mixer attachments, for at least 15 minutes. Once chilled, whip the mixture until it holds soft peaks, 3 to 5 minutes.
- Let the cake cool in the skillet on a wire rack for 10 minutes. Run a knife around the edge to loosen. If you see liquid around the edges of the skillet, carefully pour off into a measuring cup and set aside. (It's O.K. if you don't have any excess liquid — it all depends on how juicy your fruit is.)
- Carefully invert the cake onto a serving plate and drizzle with any reserved liquid. Let cool about 10 minutes more, to set. Cut into wedges using a serrated knife and serve, topping each slice with whipped cream if you like.

Nutrition Information

- 420: calories;
- 24 grams: fat;

- 15 grams: saturated fat;
- 1 gram: polyunsaturated fat;
- 7 grams: monounsaturated fat;
- 47 grams: carbohydrates;
- 2 grams: dietary fiber;
- 33 grams: sugars;
- 4 grams: protein;
- 106 milligrams: sodium;

47. Peaches In Amaretto Caramel

Serving: 4 servings | Prep: | Cook: | Ready in: 35mins

Ingredients

- 2 cups sugar
- ⅓ cup amaretto
- ¼ cup lemon juice
- 8 Small peaches, halved and pitted
- 1 cup mascarpone
- 4 tablespoons shelled, splintered pistachios, or toasted flaked almonds

Direction

- In small saucepan, combine sugar with 1 cup water. Place over low heat until sugar has dissolved. Raise heat to medium-high, and without stirring, allow syrup to bubble until it begins to caramelize and turn golden, about 20 minutes.
- Mix amaretto and lemon juice together. Reduce heat under saucepan to low. Standing back from pan, slowly pour in mixture; it will spit, then simmer. Stir to dissolve any sugar strands that have formed.
- Place peach halves in pan, in batches if necessary. Poach until just tender, 2 to 3 minutes, then transfer to plate. When all peaches have been poached, raise heat to medium-high, and boil caramel down until it is thick but still can be poured; there should be about 1 cup.
- Place 4 peach halves on each of four plates. Drizzle with caramel. Garnish each plate with a dollop of mascarpone sprinkled with splintered pistachios.

Nutrition Information

- 838: calories;
- 8 grams: monounsaturated fat;
- 3 grams: polyunsaturated fat;
- 5 grams: dietary fiber;
- 9 grams: protein;
- 27 grams: fat;
- 12 grams: saturated fat;
- 140 grams: carbohydrates;
- 132 grams: sugars;
- 211 milligrams: sodium;

48. Peanut Brittle

Serving: About 1 pound | Prep: | Cook: | Ready in: 20mins

Ingredients

- Butter for greasing pan
- 2 cups sugar
- 2 cups roasted peanuts, salted or unsalted, or other nuts
- Salt, if using unsalted peanuts (optional)

Direction

- Use a bit of butter to grease a baking sheet, preferably one with a low rim. Combine sugar and 2 tablespoons water in a heavy skillet and turn heat to medium. Stir until smooth, then cook, adjusting heat so that mixture bubbles steadily. Stir occasionally until mixture turns golden brown (which it may do rather suddenly).
- Stir in the peanuts and a large pinch of salt, if desired. Pour mixture onto greased baking sheet and spread out. Cool for about a half-hour, then break into pieces. (You can score brittle with a knife when it has solidified slightly but not yet turned hard; that way, it

will break into even squares.) Store in a covered container for up to two weeks.

Nutrition Information

- 327: calories;
- 41 grams: sugars;
- 8 grams: protein;
- 15 grams: fat;
- 45 grams: carbohydrates;
- 0 grams: trans fat;
- 7 grams: monounsaturated fat;
- 5 grams: polyunsaturated fat;
- 6 milligrams: sodium;
- 2 grams: dietary fiber;

49. Pear Pomegranate Pie

Serving: One 9-inch single pie, 8 servings | Prep: | Cook: | Ready in: 1hours30mins

Ingredients

- 4 Bosc pears (about 2 pounds), peeled and cored
- 4 Anjou pears (about 2 pounds), peeled and cored
- 6 tablespoons pomegranate molasses
- 3 tablespoons unsalted butter, cut into small pieces
- 3 tablespoons tapioca
- ¾ cup light brown sugar
- ½ teaspoon ground ginger
- ¼ teaspoon salt
- Flour, for dusting
- Dough for 2 9-inch pie crusts (see recipe)

Direction

- Preheat oven to 425 degrees. Quarter 6 pears. In a large skillet over medium-high heat, bring 3 tablespoons molasses to a boil. Let simmer about 2 minutes, until molasses thickens. Arrange half the quartered pears in a single layer in skillet. Sprinkle 1 1/2 tablespoons butter over pears. Cook, turning occasionally, until pears are well caramelized on all sides (but not cooked through), about 5 minutes.
- Scrape pears and molasses into a bowl. Add tapioca and toss to combine. Repeat cooking process with remaining molasses, butter and quartered pears. Add second batch of pears to bowl; combine.
- Thinly slice remaining pears and add to bowl. Stir in sugar, ginger and salt. On a lightly floured surface, roll out both crusts to 12-inch circles. Place one crust in 9-inch pie plate. Scrape pear filling into crust.
- Cut remaining dough into strips about 1 inch thick. Top pie with strips, weaving them into a lattice. Crimp edges to seal. Place pie on a foil-lined, rimmed baking sheet.
- Bake for 15 minutes; reduce heat to 350 degrees and continue baking until crust is dark golden and pears are tender when pricked with a fork, about 45 minutes more. Let cool for 30 minutes before slicing.

Nutrition Information

- 437: calories;
- 3 grams: saturated fat;
- 2 grams: monounsaturated fat;
- 6 grams: protein;
- 434 milligrams: sodium;
- 45 grams: sugars;
- 7 grams: fat;
- 0 grams: trans fat;
- 1 gram: polyunsaturated fat;
- 89 grams: carbohydrates;
- 8 grams: dietary fiber;

50. Pineapples Victoria

Serving: 6 servings | Prep: | Cook: | Ready in: 1hours30mins

Ingredients

- Creme brulee simple:
- 2 pints heavy cream
- Beans scraped from 2 vanilla pods
- 10 large eggs
- ½ cup granulated sugar
- ¼ cup soft light brown sugar
- ¼ cup confectioners' sugar
- Pineapple:
- 3 gorgeous small pineapples
- 4 tablespoons butter
- ⅓ cup honey
- ⅓ cup light rum

Direction

- The day before serving, make the creme brulee by preheating the oven to 325 degrees and bringing the cream and vanilla seeds to a simmer. Whisk eggs and granulated sugar until blended. Add the hot cream in a steady stream, whisking the egg mixture constantly. Pour into a 2-quart souffle dish set in a roasting pan of hot water that comes 1/4 up the side and bake about 45 minutes -- the custard should be firm but not set. Cool to room temperature and refrigerate.
- Cut pineapple in half lengthwise, scoop out flesh and chop it into bite-size pieces.
- Preheat the broiler. Melt the butter, stir in the honey and add the pineapple and its juice. Saute until liquid evaporates. Add rum, warm it and set it on fire. Divide the mixture among the 6 pineapple shells, cover each with cold creame brlee and sprinkle with the sugars. Broil until the sugars are caramelized, watching carefully.

Nutrition Information

- 1098: calories;
- 0 grams: trans fat;
- 22 grams: monounsaturated fat;
- 93 grams: carbohydrates;
- 16 grams: protein;
- 186 milligrams: sodium;
- 75 grams: fat;
- 44 grams: saturated fat;
- 4 grams: polyunsaturated fat;
- 5 grams: dietary fiber;
- 81 grams: sugars;

51. Pizza With Caramelized Onions, Figs, Bacon And Blue Cheese

Serving: Serves 2 | Prep: | Cook: |Ready in: 1hours30mins

Ingredients

- 2 tablespoons butter
- 1 large Spanish onion
- 2 teaspoons fresh thyme leaves
- 2 bay leaves
- Kosher salt
- 4 thick slices bacon, cut into 1/4-inch thick batons
- 1 ball pizza dough
- Flour, for dusting surface
- 12 dried mission figs, stems trimmed, cut into quarters or small pieces
- ¾ cup crumbled Gorgonzola
- Extra-virgin olive oil, to drizzle
- Freshly cracked black pepper

Direction

- At least 45 minutes before cooking, preheat the oven and pizza stone to 550 degrees.
- Melt the butter in a large sauté pan over high heat. Add the onions, thyme and bay leaves. Cook for 5 minutes, stirring often, until the onions begin to wilt. Reduce the heat to medium-low and cook, stirring occasionally, until the onions have softened and turn a deep, golden brown, about 25 minutes. Season to taste with salt and pepper. Remove the bay leaves and transfer the onions to a small bowl.
- Place the bacon in the pan and set over high heat. Cook, stirring occasionally, until brown and crispy. Using a slotted spoon, transfer the bacon to a small bowl.

- Place the pizza dough on a heavily floured surface and stretch and pull, using your hands or a rolling pin, into about a 14-inch round. Place on a lightly floured pizza peel or rimless baking sheet. Cover with the toppings, careful not to press on the dough and weigh it down: the caramelized onions first, then the figs and bacon, and finally the Gorgonzola, leaving roughly a 1/2 inch border. Shake the pizza peel slightly to make sure the dough is not sticking. Carefully slide the pizza directly onto the baking stone in one quick, forward-and-back motion. Cook until the crust has browned on the bottom and the top is bubbling and browning in spots, about 7 minutes. Drizzle with a little olive oil and some cracked black pepper. Serve hot. Makes 1 pizza.

Nutrition Information

- 1193: calories;
- 32 grams: protein;
- 1671 milligrams: sodium;
- 27 grams: saturated fat;
- 131 grams: carbohydrates;
- 14 grams: dietary fiber;
- 24 grams: monounsaturated fat;
- 8 grams: polyunsaturated fat;
- 55 grams: sugars;
- 63 grams: fat;
- 1 gram: trans fat;

52. Pizza With Caramelized Onions, Ricotta And Chard

Serving: One 14-inch pizza (eight slices) | Prep: | Cook: | Ready in: 1hours30mins

Ingredients

- 2 tablespoons extra virgin olive oil
- 1 ¼ pounds onions, sliced
- 1 teaspoon chopped fresh thyme leaves
- 2 garlic cloves, minced
- Salt
- freshly ground pepper
- ½ pound chard, stemmed, leaves washed
- 1 14-inch pizza crust (1/2 batch pizza dough)
- ¾ cup ricotta (6 ounces)
- 2 ounces Parmesan, grated 1/2 cup, tightly packed
- 1 egg yolk

Direction

- Thirty minutes before baking the pizza, preheat the oven to 500 degrees. Heat the olive oil over medium heat in a large, heavy skillet. Add the onions. Cook, stirring often, until tender and just beginning to color, about 10 minutes. Add the thyme, garlic and a generous pinch of salt. Turn the heat to low, cover and cook another 10 to 20 minutes, stirring often, until the onions are golden brown and very sweet and soft. Remove from the heat.
- While the onions are cooking, stem and wash the chard leaves, and bring a medium pot of water to a boil. Fill a medium bowl with ice water. When the water comes to a boil, salt generously and add the chard. Blanch for one to two minutes, just until the leaves are tender, and transfer to the ice water. Drain and squeeze out excess water. Alternatively, steam the chard for two to three minutes until wilted, and rinse with cold water. Chop the chard medium-fine.
- Roll out the dough, oil a 14-inch pizza pan and dust with cornmeal or semolina. Place the dough on the pan.
- In a medium bowl, combine the ricotta, egg yolk, Parmesan and chard. Spread over the pizza dough in an even layer, leaving a 1-inch border around the rim. Spread the onions over the ricotta mixture.
- Place in the hot oven, and bake 10 to 15 minutes until the crust and bits of the onion are nicely browned. Remove from the heat, and serve hot or warm.

Nutrition Information

- 213: calories;
- 10 grams: fat;
- 4 grams: sugars;
- 1 gram: polyunsaturated fat;
- 23 grams: carbohydrates;
- 3 grams: dietary fiber;
- 9 grams: protein;
- 378 milligrams: sodium;

53. Pizza With Spring Onions And Fennel

Serving: One 12- to 14-inch pizza | Prep: | Cook: | Ready in: 45mins

Ingredients

- 2 tablespoons extra virgin olive oil
- 1 medium size sweet spring onion, chopped, about 1 cup
- Salt, preferably kosher salt
- freshly ground pepper
- 1 ¼ pounds trimmed fennel bulbs, tough outer layers removed, cored and chopped
- 2 large garlic cloves, minced
- 2 tablespoons minced fennel fronds
- ½ recipe whole wheat pizza dough (see recipe)
- Parmesan

Direction

- Preheat the oven to 450 degrees, preferably with a baking stone in it. Heat 1 tablespoon of the olive oil over medium heat in a large, heavy skillet, and add the onion and about 1/2 teaspoon salt. Cook, stirring often, until the onion is tender, about five minutes. Add the fennel and garlic, and stir together. Cook, stirring often, until the fennel begins to soften, about five minutes. Turn the heat to low, cover and cook gently, stirring often, until the fennel is very tender and sweet and just beginning to color, about 15 minutes. Season to taste with salt and pepper. Stir in the chopped fennel fronds, and remove from the heat.
- Roll or press out the pizza dough and line a 12- to 14-inch pan. Brush the pizza crust with the remaining tablespoon of olive oil and sprinkle on the Parmesan. Spread the fennel mixture over the crust in an even layer. Place on top of the pizza stone, and bake 15 to 20 minutes, until the edges of the crust are brown and the topping is beginning to brown. Remove from the heat. Serve hot, warm or room temperature.

54. Praline

Serving: Two cups | Prep: | Cook: | Ready in: 25mins

Ingredients

- 1 cup sugar
- ¼ cup water
- ¾ cup whole blanched almonds
- 1 tablespoon corn, peanut or other unflavored vegetable oil

Direction

- Combine the sugar and water in a saucepan and bring to the boil. Cook over moderately high heat for five minutes.
- Stir in the almonds and continue cooking, stirring almost constantly with a wire whisk. The syrup will become granular for a brief time. Continue cooking for a total of about five minutes or until the syrup becomes a dark caramel color.
- Meanwhile, brush a cold flat surface (preferably marble or glass, not wood) with oil and wipe with a paper towel to leave a light film of oil. Pour the caramelized almonds onto the surface. Let stand until thoroughly cold. The praline may be cracked and eaten at this point. Or it may be pulverized.
- Break up the caramelized almonds into pieces. Pulverize the pieces. This may be done two ways, using a rolling pin (which is more traditional) or a food processor. If you use a

food processor, a little oil might come out of the almonds.

Nutrition Information

- 257: calories;
- 12 grams: fat;
- 0 grams: trans fat;
- 8 grams: monounsaturated fat;
- 37 grams: carbohydrates;
- 34 grams: sugars;
- 4 grams: protein;
- 4 milligrams: sodium;
- 3 grams: polyunsaturated fat;
- 2 grams: dietary fiber;
- 1 gram: saturated fat;

55. Praline Pear Cake

Serving: 6 servings | Prep: | Cook: | Ready in: 1hours

Ingredients

- 2 tablespoons slivered almonds
- ⅓ cup plus 1/2 cup sugar
- 3 tablespoons water
- 2 ripe but firm Bosc or D'Anjou pears
- 4 tablespoons unsalted butter, softened
- 1 egg
- ⅔ cup flour
- ½ teaspoon baking powder
- ½ teaspoon almond extract
- Whipped cream

Direction

- Preheat oven to 350 degrees. Butter an eight-inch round cake pan but do not use one with a removable bottom.
- Toast the almonds until lightly browned under the broiler, in a toaster oven or in a heavy ungreased skillet on the top of the stove. Set aside.
- Swirl one-third cup of the sugar with the water in a heavy saucepan or skillet until the sugar dissolves. Place over medium heat and cook, stirring occasionally, until the mixture turns a uniform honey-brown color. Pour the caramel into the cake pan, tilting it so the caramel coats the bottom. Immediately scatter the almonds over the caramel.
- Peel and core the pears. Cut them into thin, uniform slices and arrange the slices, overlapping, in a pattern on top of the caramel and almonds.
- Cream the butter with one-half cup of sugar. Beat in the egg. Sift the flour and baking powder together and stir into the batter. Add the almond extract.
- Spread the batter over the pears in the cakepan. There will be a thin layer of batter. A spatula moistened in cold water will make spreading it easier.
- Place in preheated oven and bake for 30 minutes. Remove from oven, allow to cool for a minute or two, run a knife around the edge, then unmold onto a serving dish. If any of the topping clings to the pan, lift it off and replace it on the cake. Serve the cake while still warm with whipped cream.

Nutrition Information

- 286: calories;
- 3 grams: protein;
- 1 gram: polyunsaturated fat;
- 49 grams: carbohydrates;
- 43 milligrams: sodium;
- 10 grams: fat;
- 5 grams: saturated fat;
- 0 grams: trans fat;
- 34 grams: sugars;

56. Provençal Onion Pizza

Serving: One 12- to 14 inch pizza | Prep: | Cook: | Ready in: 1hours15mins

Ingredients

- 3 tablespoons olive oil
- 2 pounds sweet onions, finely chopped
- Salt
- freshly ground pepper
- 3 garlic cloves, minced
- ½ bay leaf
- 2 teaspoons fresh thyme leaves, or 1 teaspoon dried thyme
- 1 tablespoon capers, drained, rinsed and mashed in a mortar and pestle or finely chopped
- ½ recipe whole wheat pizza dough (see recipe)
- 12 anchovy fillets, soaked in water for five minutes, drained, rinsed and dried on paper towels
- 12 Niçoise olives

Direction

- Preheat the oven to 450 degrees, preferably with a pizza stone inside. Heat 2 tablespoons of the olive oil in a large, heavy nonstick skillet over medium-low heat. Add the onions and cook, stirring, until they begin to sizzle and soften, about three minutes. Add a generous pinch of salt and the garlic, bay leaf, thyme and pepper. Stir everything together, turn the heat to low, cover and cook slowly for 45 minutes, stirring often. The onions should melt down to a golden brown puree. If they begin to stick, add a few tablespoons of water. Stir in the capers, then taste and adjust seasonings. If there is liquid in the pan, cook over medium heat, uncovered, until it evaporates.
- Roll out the pizza dough and line a 12- to 14-inch pan. Brush the remaining tablespoon of oil over the bottom but not the rim of the crust. Spread the onions over the crust in an even layer. Cut the anchovies in half, and decorate the top of the crust with them, making twelve small X's and placing an olive in the middle of each X. Place on top of the pizza stone, and bake 15 to 20 minutes, until the edges of the crust are brown and the onions are beginning to brown. Remove from the heat. Serve hot, warm or room temperature.

Nutrition Information

- 189: calories;
- 9 grams: fat;
- 1 gram: polyunsaturated fat;
- 6 grams: monounsaturated fat;
- 23 grams: carbohydrates;
- 5 grams: protein;
- 2 grams: dietary fiber;
- 8 grams: sugars;
- 503 milligrams: sodium;

57. Pumpkin Flan

Serving: 10 to 12 servings | Prep: | Cook: |Ready in: 2hours

Ingredients

- 1 ¾ cups/350 grams granulated sugar, divided
- 1 cinnamon stick
- 2 cups/473 milliliters half-and-half
- 4 large eggs, plus 2 large egg yolks
- 1 teaspoon pure vanilla extract
- ½ teaspoon pumpkin pie spice (see note)
- ⅛ teaspoon fine salt
- ½ cup/125 grams pumpkin purée (from a speckled hound, calabaza or other cooking pumpkin)
- ½ cup/125 grams butternut squash purée (see note)

Direction

- Make the caramel: In a heavy saucepan, mix 3/4 cup sugar and 1/4 cup water. The mixture should look like wet sand. Cook over medium heat, stirring frequently, until it begins to make large bubbles. Continue to cook without stirring, rotating the pan regularly, until the caramel is translucent and amber-colored, 12 to 15 minutes. Working quickly, pour caramel

- into a 2-quart oven-safe glass bowl and rotate the bowl so it coats the sides.
- Make the flan: In another saucepan, combine remaining sugar, cinnamon stick and half-and-half. Cook over medium heat, stirring occasionally, until sugar is dissolved, about 5 minutes. Let cool.
- Heat oven to 350 degrees. Whisk eggs and egg yolks in a large bowl until well blended. Whisk in vanilla, pumpkin pie spice, salt and pumpkin and squash purées. Add cooled cream mixture and whisk well.
- Pour custard mixture through a mesh sieve, stirring and pressing with a spatula. You can do this directly into the bowl with the caramel, or into a separate bowl first, and then pour the strained mixture into the bowl with the caramel.
- Place the bowl with the custard into a larger baking dish and carefully add warm water until it reaches halfway up the sides of the flan bowl. Cover with foil and bake for 30 minutes. Remove foil and bake for another 45 to 60 minutes, or until flan is just set in the middle, but still jiggles slightly. (A wider, shallower baking vessel will cook more quickly than a deeper one.)
- Remove flan from water bath and let cool to room temperature. Refrigerate until completely cool, preferably overnight. To serve, run a knife around the edges of the flan, then put a serving platter on top of the bowl and invert. The flan should slip easily onto the serving platter with the caramel sauce pooling nicely around it.

Nutrition Information

- 208: calories;
- 7 grams: fat;
- 1 gram: dietary fiber;
- 32 grams: sugars;
- 4 grams: protein;
- 0 grams: trans fat;
- 2 grams: monounsaturated fat;
- 33 grams: carbohydrates;
- 67 milligrams: sodium;

58. Rawia Bishara's Vegetarian Musaqa

Serving: 8 servings | Prep: | Cook: | Ready in: 1hours

Ingredients

- 3 hefty eggplants, peeled, sliced lengthwise about 1/4-inch thick
- 3 tablespoons plus 1 teaspoon salt
- 4 or 5 large yellow onions, cubed or thinly sliced
- 1 ½ cups extra virgin olive oil (see note below)
- ½ cup slivered blanched almonds
- ½ cup pine nuts
- 1 large bunch fresh cilantro, coarsely chopped
- 1 tablespoon garlic, very finely minced 1 teaspoon ground cumin
- 1 teaspoon ground coriander
- 1 tablespoon ground black pepper
- ½ teaspoon ground allspice
- ¼ teaspoon ground nutmeg
- ½ cup lemon juice plus 2 more lemons
- 2 or 3 large yellow potatoes, peeled, very thinly sliced
- 4 Arab squash (kousa) or zucchini, sliced lengthwise 1/4-inch thick
- 2 fresh ripe tomatoes, thinly sliced
- 2 large red or yellow sweet peppers, coarsely chopped

Direction

- Combine eggplant with 3 tablespoons of salt in bowl and cover with cool water. Set plate on top and weight to keep eggplant submerged. Set aside for 30 to 60 minutes.
- Set aside a half-cup of onion for topping. Combine remainder with a quarter-cup of oil in a heavy skillet and set over low heat. Cook, stirring occasionally, until onions are pale caramel and very soft, almost melted into oil, 20 to 30 minutes (watch carefully to prevent

burning). Transfer to a bowl, leaving as much oil in the skillet as possible.
- Meanwhile, toast almonds in 1 tablespoon of oil in small skillet over medium-low heat until golden and crisp. Remove and add to onions. Add pine nuts to the skillet, with a little more oil if necessary, and toast until golden. Remove and add to onions.
- In same skillet, add another tablespoon of oil and toss the cilantro with garlic until wilted. Add to onion and nut mixture, with a heaping tablespoon of the spice mixture (cumin, coriander, black pepper, allspice and nutmeg) and lemon juice. Stir to mix well. Taste, adding more spices or lemon juice, if desired.
- Heat oven to 375 degrees.
- Add another half-cup of oil to skillet in which onions were cooked and set over medium-low heat. When oil is hot, add potato slices. Cook on both sides until they are lightly golden and start to soften. Transfer to 9-x-12-inch oven dish. Line bottom of dish. Distribute a fourth of the onion mixture over the top; it will not cover the potatoes.
- While potatoes are cooking, drain eggplant and dry with paper towels. Add more oil to skillet, if necessary, and cook eggplant slices on both sides until lightly golden. Use half the slices to cover the bottom layer, setting aside the other half. Distribute another quarter of onion mixture over eggplant.
- In skillet cook squash or zucchini slices on both sides until lightly golden (add more oil if needed). Arrange over eggplant and distribute some of remaining onion mixture on top. Top with reserved eggplant slices and remaining onion mixture.
- Arrange tomato slices on top, then sprinkle with peppers. Distribute reserved half onion over the top. Sprinkle with salt, and squeeze the juice of one lemon over it. Add about a half-cup boiling water, dribbling down around edges of pan. Transfer to oven and bake 20 to 30 minutes, or until top is starting to crisp and juices are bubbling.
- Remove from oven and serve immediately; or set aside to cool to slightly above room temperature before serving.

Nutrition Information

- 679: calories;
- 7 grams: saturated fat;
- 9 grams: polyunsaturated fat;
- 51 grams: carbohydrates;
- 10 grams: protein;
- 1456 milligrams: sodium;
- 0 grams: trans fat;
- 34 grams: monounsaturated fat;
- 13 grams: dietary fiber;
- 17 grams: sugars;
- 52 grams: fat;

59. Rhineland Sauerbraten

Serving: 8 to 10 servings | Prep: | Cook: |Ready in: 4hours45mins

Ingredients

- 5 pound rump of beef (top or bottom round can be used but they are not quite as good)
- ½ pound salt pork for larding
- 2 teaspoons salt
- 3 cups wine vinegar (approximately)
- 3 cups water (approximately)
- 1 large onion, sliced
- 2 bay leaves
- 8 cloves
- 8 peppercorns
- 1 tablespoon pickling spices
- 1 large carrot, scraped and sliced
- 4 slices bacon
- 2 tablespoons butter
- 2 large onions, sliced
- 1 bay leaf
- 6 cloves
- 3 tablespoons flour
- 2 tablespoons sugar

- lemon juice to taste
- ½ cup white raisins, soaked in warm water
- Tomato puree or sour cream (optional)

Direction

- Rump or round of beef should be well larded with thin matchstick strips of bacon or salt pork. Tie meat firmly with string in several places so it will be easy to turn without piercing and will hold shape. Rub well with salt on all sides and place in deep, closefitting glass or earthenware bowl.
- Combine vinegar and water and add onion, bay leaves, cloves, peppercorns, pickling spices and carrot. Bring to boil and simmer 5 minutes. Cool marinade thoroughly and pour over beef. Meat should be completely covered by marinade; if it is not, add equal amounts of water and vinegar until it is. Cover and place in refrigerator for 3 to 5 days; the longer it stands the more piquant the roast will be, so adjust time to suit taste. Turn meat in marinade 2 or 3 times a day, using string as handle.
- Remove meat from marinade. Strain marinade and reserve. Dry meat thoroughly with paper towels. Meat will not brown properly if it is wet, so dry as much as possible.
- Dice bacon and fry slowly in butter in 5-quart Dutch oven or casserole. When fat is hot, add meat and brown slowly. Using string as handle, turn so meat is well seared and golden brown (but not black) on all sides. This should take about 15 minutes.
- Remove browned meat and add sliced onions to hot fat. Fry, stirring from time to time, until onions are deep golden brown but not black.
- Return meat to pot, placing on top of onions. Add marinade until it reaches about halfway up sides of meat. Add fresh bay leaf and cloves (not those used in marinade). Bring marinade to boil, cover pot tightly with heavy, close-fitting lid, reduce heat and simmer very slowly but steadily 3 1/2 to 4 hours, turning meat 2 or 3 times during cooking. Add more marinade to pot if needed. If you cannot lower heat enough to keep sauce at slow simmer, place an asbestos mat or flame trivet under pot. Meat is done when it can be pierced easily with long-pronged fork or skewer.
- Remove meat to heated platter and strain gravy. Skim off excess fat and return gravy to pot. Melt butter in saucepan and when hot, stir in flour and sugar. Cook over very low heat, stirring constantly until sugar mixture turns a deep caramel color. Be very careful doing this, as sugar burns all at once (if it become black, this part of the operation would have to be started again). Add sugar-flour to hot gravy and stir through briskly with wire whisk.
- Season with lemon juice to taste; gravy should have a mild sweet-sour flavor. Add raisins, which have been soaked and drained. Return meat to pot, cover and simmer 10 minutes. If sauce becomes too thick, add a little more marinade. Tablespoonful of tomato puree can be stirred in and heated 4 or 5 minutes before serving time, to enrich the color of the gravy. Check gravy for seasoning. Slice meat and arrange on heated platter and mask with a little gravy, serving rest in heated sauceboat. Serve with dumplings, noodles, boiled potatoes or potato pancakes.

Nutrition Information

- 609: calories;
- 17 grams: monounsaturated fat;
- 16 grams: carbohydrates;
- 53 grams: protein;
- 36 grams: fat;
- 14 grams: saturated fat;
- 1 gram: dietary fiber;
- 4 grams: polyunsaturated fat;
- 9 grams: sugars;
- 1096 milligrams: sodium;

60. Rigatoni And Cauliflower Al Forno

Serving: 4 to 6 servings | Prep: | Cook: | Ready in: 1hours

Ingredients

- 1 pound rigatoni or other large pasta shape
- 1 medium cauliflower, about 1 1/2 pounds
- Extra-virgin olive oil
- Salt and pepper
- 1 tablespoon capers, roughly chopped
- 3 garlic cloves, minced
- ¼ teaspoon crushed red pepper flakes, or more to taste
- 3 tablespoons roughly chopped sage, plus a few sage leaves left whole
- ½ teaspoon lemon zest
- 6 ounces coarsely grated fontina or mozzarella
- 2 ounces finely grated Romano cheese or other hard pecorino
- ½ cup coarse dry bread crumbs
- 2 tablespoons chopped flat-leaf parsley, for garnish

Direction

- Cook the rigatoni in well-salted water according to package directions, but drain while still quite al dente. (If directions call for 12 minutes cooking, cook for 10 instead.) Rinse pasta with cool water, then drain again and set aside.
- Heat oven to 400 degrees. Cut cauliflower in half from top to bottom. Cut out tough core and stem any extraneous leaves. Lay cauliflower flat side down and cut crosswise into rough 1/4-inch slices. Break into smaller pieces.
- Put 3 tablespoons olive oil in a wide skillet over high heat. Add cauliflower slices, along with any crumbly pieces, in one layer. (Work in batches if necessary.) Let cauliflower brown and caramelize for about 2 minutes, then turn pieces over to brown the other side. Cook for another 2 minutes, or until the cauliflower is easily pierced with a fork. It's fine if some pieces don't brown evenly. Season generously with salt and pepper. Add capers, garlic, red pepper flakes, chopped sage, sage leaves and lemon zest and stir to coat.
- Put cooked cauliflower mixture in a large mixing bowl. Add cooked rigatoni and fontina and toss. Transfer mixture to a lightly oiled baking dish. Top with Romano cheese, then with bread crumbs and drizzle with about 1 tablespoon olive oil. (Dish may be completed to this point up to several hours in advance and kept at room temperature, covered.)
- Bake, uncovered, for about 20 minutes, until top is crisp and golden. Sprinkle with freshly chopped parsley before serving.

Nutrition Information

- 521: calories;
- 575 milligrams: sodium;
- 6 grams: dietary fiber;
- 70 grams: carbohydrates;
- 4 grams: sugars;
- 23 grams: protein;
- 17 grams: fat;
- 8 grams: saturated fat;
- 2 grams: polyunsaturated fat;

61. Roasted Blood Oranges

Serving: 2 servings | Prep: | Cook: | Ready in: 4hours30mins

Ingredients

- 10 fresh mint leaves
- 1 egg white, lightly beaten, optional
- ¼ cup granulated sugar, optional
- 4 blood oranges
- ½ cup Demerara (granulated light brown) sugar
- A few drops of mint oil

Direction

- If crystallizing the mint leaves, place them on a sheet of parchment paper. Brush lightly with egg white on both sides. Place sugar in a small mound and dip each coated leaf in the sugar, to cover both sides. Shake off excess. Place leaves on a plate to dry for about 4 hours or in a turned-off oven with a pilot light, until dry and crisp.
- Peel oranges, removing all pith. Cut each in 4 slices horizontally, removing any seeds. Refrigerate at least 2 hours. Place Demerara sugar on a plate and dip each orange slice in the sugar on one side. Use a butane or propane torch, or light a broiler with the rack as close as possible to the heat element. On a baking sheet lined with foil, place oranges, sugared side up. Use the torch to caramelize the sugar, or place slices under the broiler until the edges are seared. Allow to cool briefly, then coat with sugar and sear again. Place slices on a cooling rack and allow to sit at least 1 hour.
- Arrange slices on individual plates. Dot with a few drops of mint oil, garnish with the plain or sugared mint leaves and serve.

Nutrition Information

- 261: calories;
- 66 grams: carbohydrates;
- 6 grams: dietary fiber;
- 60 grams: sugars;
- 3 grams: protein;
- 10 milligrams: sodium;
- 0 grams: polyunsaturated fat;

62. Roseanne Gold's Pumpkin Flan

Serving: Six servings | Prep: | Cook: | Ready in: 1hours40mins

Ingredients

- 1 ¼ cups sugar
- ½ teaspoon salt
- 1 teaspoon ground cinnamon
- 1 cup cooked pumpkin
- 5 eggs, lightly beaten
- 1 ½ cups evaporated milk
- ⅓ cup water
- 1 ½ teaspoons vanilla

Direction

- Preheat oven to 350 degrees.
- In a heavy-bottom fry pan, melt a half cup of sugar, stirring constantly, until it caramelizes.
- Pour caramelized sugar into individual custard cups or a glass loaf pan.
- Combine sugar with salt and cinnamon. Add pumpkin and eggs. Mix well. Stir in milk, water and vanilla.
- Pour mixture into custard cups or loaf pan. Set in hot water bath.
- Bake for 1 1/4 hours. Chill.
- To serve, turn the cups or pan upside down to obtain the handsome hues of the pumpkin glaze.

Nutrition Information

- 306: calories;
- 0 grams: dietary fiber;
- 50 grams: carbohydrates;
- 49 grams: sugars;
- 313 milligrams: sodium;
- 8 grams: fat;
- 4 grams: saturated fat;
- 3 grams: monounsaturated fat;
- 1 gram: polyunsaturated fat;
- 9 grams: protein;

63. Salted Butter Caramels

Serving: Makes 128 caramels | Prep: | Cook: | Ready in: 1hours

Ingredients

- Vegetable oil
- 1 ⅓ cups heavy cream
- 2 cups sugar
- ½ cup light corn syrup
- ⅓ cup honey
- 6 tablespoons unsalted butter, cubed
- 1 teaspoon vanilla paste or extract
- 3 teaspoons fleur de sel or sea salt
- 1 ½ pounds bittersweet chocolate, finely chopped

Direction

- Line an 8-by-8-inch baking pan with aluminum foil that extends over the sides. Grease with vegetable oil. In a heavy 4-quart saucepan, bring the cream to a boil. Add the sugar, corn syrup and honey and stir constantly with a wooden spoon until the mixture comes to a boil. Cook, stirring occasionally, until the mixture reaches 257 degrees on a candy thermometer, 15 to 30 minutes.
- Remove the pan from the heat and, with oven mitts on, stir in the butter, vanilla and 2 teaspoons salt. Pour into the prepared pan and let cool. If you are not coating them in chocolate, let cool slightly and sprinkle with the remaining salt. When completely cool, coat a cutting board and the blade of a large chef's knife with vegetable oil. Invert the caramel onto the cutting board; peel off the foil and invert again. Cut the caramel into 8 1-inch-wide strips; then cut each strip into 1/2-inch pieces.
- To coat with chocolate, melt the chocolate in a double boiler (temper it if you want the coating to have polish; directions can be found at www.baking 911.com). Using a fork to hold the caramel pieces, dip them one at a time into the chocolate and set them on a rack to cool. After dipping 4 caramels, sprinkle each with a little of the remaining sea salt. Transfer to parchment paper to set up and cool.

Nutrition Information

- 59: calories;
- 3 grams: fat;
- 2 grams: saturated fat;
- 0 grams: protein;
- 1 gram: monounsaturated fat;
- 8 grams: sugars;
- 33 milligrams: sodium;

64. Sausage Ragù

Serving: About 3 cups | Prep: | Cook: | Ready in: 2hours

Ingredients

- 1 pound sweet Italian sausage or bulk sausage
- Extra-virgin olive oil
- 1 onion, minced
- 1 carrot, minced
- 1 celery stalk, minced
- ¼ cup minced flat-leaf parsley, plus extra for garnish
- 1 28-ounce can whole tomatoes, preferably San Marzano, with its juice
- 1 large sprig fresh thyme
- 1 large sprig fresh rosemary
- 3 tablespoons tomato paste
- Salt
- Ground black pepper
- 1 pound tubular dried pasta such as mezzi rigatoni, paccheri or penne
- Freshly grated Parmesan cheese, for garnish, optional

Direction

- With the tip of a small, sharp knife, slit open the sausage casings. Crumble the meat into a wide, heavy skillet or Dutch oven and set over medium-low heat. If the meat is not rendering enough fat to coat the bottom of the pan as it begins to cook, add olive oil one tablespoon at a time until the meat is frying gently, not steaming. Sauté, breaking up any large chunks, until all the meat has turned opaque (do not let it brown), about 5 minutes.

- Add onion, carrot, celery and parsley and stir. Drizzle in more oil if the pan seems dry. Cook over very low heat, stirring often, until the vegetables have melted in the fat and are beginning to caramelize, and the meat is toasty brown. This may take as long as 40 minutes, but be patient: It is essential to the final flavors.
- Add tomatoes and their juice, breaking up the tomatoes with your hands or with the side of a spoon. Bring to a simmer, then add thyme and rosemary and let simmer, uncovered, until thickened and pan is almost dry, 20 to 25 minutes.
- Mix tomato paste with 1 cup hot water. Add to pan, reduce heat to very low, and continue cooking until the ragù is velvety and dark red, and the top glistens with oil, about 10 minutes more. Remove herb sprigs. Sprinkle black pepper over, stir and taste.
- Meanwhile, bring a large pot of salted water to a boil. Boil pasta until just tender. Scoop out 2 cups cooking water, drain pasta and return to pot over low heat. Quickly add a ladleful of ragù, a splash of cooking water, stir well and let cook 1 minute. Taste for doneness. Repeat, adding more cooking water or ragù, or both, until pasta is cooked through and seasoned to your liking.
- Pour hot pasta water into a large serving bowl to heat it. Pour out the water and pour in the pasta. Top with remaining ragù, sprinkle with parsley and serve immediately. Pass grated cheese at the table, if desired.

Nutrition Information

- 276: calories;
- 321 milligrams: sodium;
- 3 grams: sugars;
- 0 grams: trans fat;
- 5 grams: monounsaturated fat;
- 2 grams: dietary fiber;
- 11 grams: protein;
- 12 grams: fat;
- 32 grams: carbohydrates;

65. Seared Albacore And Peaches With Quinoa, Haricots Verts And Pistou

Serving: 4 servings | Prep: | Cook: | Ready in: 45mins

Ingredients

- ½ cup quinoa
- 2 tablespoons extra virgin olive oil
- Salt
- 2 cups haricots verts
- 2 cups firmly packed fresh basil leaves
- 1 cup firmly packed fresh parsley leaves
- ¼ cup firmly packed fresh tarragon leaves
- 2 cloves garlic, minced
- ¾ cup plus 1 tablespoon grapeseed oil
- 3 to 4 tablespoons fresh lemon juice, or as needed
- 2 peaches, halved and pitted
- 1 ½ pounds fresh albacore tuna
- Black pepper

Direction

- In a medium saucepan, combine quinoa with 2 cups water. Bring to a boil, then reduce heat to low and simmer, covered, until all the water is absorbed, 10 to 15 minutes. Remove from heat, add olive oil, and toss to mix. Cover and keep warm.
- Place a large pot of lightly salted water over high heat to bring to a boil. Set aside a large bowl filled with water and ice.
- Add haricots verts to boiling water and blanch just until bright green, about 30 seconds. Using a slotted spoon, scoop out beans (reserving boiling water) and transfer to ice water to chill. Using the slotted spoon, transfer beans to a colander (reserving ice water) and drain.
- Add basil, parsley and tarragon to boiling water. Blanch 2 minutes, then drain and transfer to ice water to chill. Drain again. Place

herbs in a kitchen towel and roll gently to remove excess water. Chop coarsely and place in a blender. Add garlic and 1/2 cup grapeseed oil. Blend until very smooth. Place haricot verts in a bowl, and toss with 2 tablespoons of the herb purée (known as pistou) and lemon juice to taste, reserving remaining pistou and juice.
- Place a large sauté pan over medium heat, and add 1/4 cup grapeseed oil. Sear peaches, cut sides down, until caramelized and golden brown, about 3 minutes, then remove from heat and set aside. Clean pan and return to high heat. Add remaining 1 tablespoon grapeseed oil. Season tuna with salt and pepper to taste. Add to pan and sear sides and edges so the center remains raw, 30 seconds to 1 minute each side, pressing tuna against side of pan to sear edges. Remove from heat, slice thinly, and season with lemon juice and salt to taste.
- To serve, spread quinoa across 4 serving plates. Top with haricot verts mixture. Arrange peach halves on top. Fan the sliced tuna on the plates, and garnish with pistou as desired.

Nutrition Information

- 915: calories;
- 9 grams: sugars;
- 961 milligrams: sodium;
- 8 grams: saturated fat;
- 18 grams: monounsaturated fat;
- 29 grams: carbohydrates;
- 5 grams: dietary fiber;
- 67 grams: fat;
- 38 grams: polyunsaturated fat;
- 51 grams: protein;

66. Seared Scallops With Hot Sauce Beurre Blanc

Serving: 4 servings | Prep: | Cook: | Ready in: 30mins

Ingredients

- For the salsa:
- 1 large shallot, finely chopped
- ¼ cup finely chopped fennel fronds
- 1 cup chopped cherry tomatoes
- 1 tablespoon extra-virgin olive oil
- 1 teaspoon red wine vinegar
- For the scallops:
- 1 pound large dry-processed sea scallops (about 12)
- Kosher salt and black pepper
- 2 tablespoons grapeseed or canola oil
- 2 tablespoons white wine
- Juice of 1 large lemon
- ¼ cup Crystal hot sauce (Frank's or Texas Pete's can be substituted; do not use Tabasco)
- 2 sticks (1/2 pound) chilled butter, cut into cubes

Direction

-
-

Nutrition Information

- 616: calories;
- 15 grams: protein;
- 832 milligrams: sodium;
- 30 grams: saturated fat;
- 2 grams: dietary fiber;
- 19 grams: monounsaturated fat;
- 4 grams: sugars;
- 12 grams: carbohydrates;
- 57 grams: fat;

67. Singaporean Braised Duck

Serving: 6 servings | Prep: | Cook: |Ready in: 1hours15mins

Ingredients

- 1 5-pound duck, whole
- 2 tablespoons kosher salt, plus more to taste
- 2 tablespoons Chinese five-spice powder
- 8 teaspoons sugar
- 4 pods star anise
- 15 cloves garlic, lightly smashed
- 4 inches galangal or ginger, peeled and sliced into 1/4-inch coins
- 1 cup kecap manis (see note)
- 14 ounces packaged fried tofu, cut into 2-inch pieces
- 6 hard-boiled eggs
- Steamed rice, for serving
- Auntie Khar Imm's Chile Sauce (see recipe)

Direction

- Trim the duck of any visible excess fat, especially from the tail area. Mix together the salt and five-spice powder, and season the duck all over, including inside the cavity, and marinate, refrigerated, for 2 hours or overnight. Rinse the duck with fresh water inside and out.
- Place a large wok or Dutch oven over medium heat, and add the sugar. After it liquefies, watch it carefully as it caramelizes to a medium brown, swirling the pot occasionally to help it color evenly. Add the star anise, garlic and ginger, and stir to coat in the caramel, and to keep the caramel cooking until it's a dark brown, but not burned. Stir in 1 cup of water to dissolve the caramel, then add the kecap manis.
- Add duck, breast side up, then add water to come up halfway, submerging the legs. Raise the heat to bring the liquid to a boil, then turn the heat down to a very gentle simmer, just barely bubbling.
- Cook for 15 minutes, then carefully flip the duck so the breast side is down. Cook 15 minutes, then flip again. Taste the liquid, and add salt or more kecap manis to taste. Cook 15 minutes, then flip so the breast side is down again. Cook another 5 to 15 minutes, until the breast is cooked to your liking. Traditionally it should be cooked through, but Tan's spin is to remove the duck when the breast meat is 135 to 140 degrees, or medium. To use a traditional test, poke a chopstick in the thickest parts of the duck thigh and breast; if it goes through without too much resistance, it's done.
- Remove the duck to a platter or cutting board, and tent with foil. Let it rest for 10 minutes. Add the tofu and eggs to the sauce, and simmer them gently for 10 minutes, until stained and hot. Skim the sauce of any floating fat if necessary, and serve it all with rice and chile sauce.

Nutrition Information

- 1281: calories;
- 115 grams: fat;
- 54 grams: monounsaturated fat;
- 16 grams: carbohydrates;
- 2 grams: dietary fiber;
- 38 grams: saturated fat;
- 7 grams: sugars;
- 46 grams: protein;
- 2568 milligrams: sodium;

68. Sliced Oranges With Pomegranate Caramelized Walnuts

Serving: 4 servings | Prep: | Cook: |Ready in: 20mins

Ingredients

- 3 Valencia oranges, scrubbed well, skin on
- 1 cup shelled walnuts, about 4 ounces
- ½ cup sugar

- Juice from 1 large or 2 small ripe pomegranates (about 1/2 cup)
- Seeds from 1/2 small pomegranate (about 1/4 cup)

Direction

- Trim ends from oranges, and discard. Thinly slice the oranges crosswise. Discard seeds. Lay 5 slices of orange on each of 4 plates, and set aside.
- Place walnuts in 10-inch nonstick pan over medium-high heat. After about 2 1/2 minutes, they will begin to make popping sounds. Continue to cook, stirring and turning the nuts, until they are crisp and the edges are brown, about 2 1/2 more minutes.
- Sprinkle sugar evenly over nuts. Let sugar sit until it begins to melt, and then start to stir. Continue to cook, stirring, until sugar completely melts, turns a dark golden caramel color and coats the nuts, about 3 1/2 minutes.
- Stir in the pomegranate juice. Cook, stirring vigorously, for 30 seconds. Remove nuts from heat, and continue to stir for 1 or 2 minutes to cool. Divide the warm gooey nuts evenly over the oranges. Sprinkle with pomegranate seeds, and serve.

69. Smoked Trout In Caramelized Apple And Onion Broth

Serving: Four servings | Prep: | Cook: |Ready in: 2hours10mins

Ingredients

- 2 teaspoons unsalted butter
- 2 large onions, peeled, halved lengthwise and thinly sliced
- 4 Granny Smith apples, cored and thinly sliced
- ¼ cup dry sherry
- 6 cups water
- ½ cup finely diced, stemmed shiitake mushrooms
- ½ cup finely diced, peeled butternut squash
- ½ cup finely diced, peeled carrot
- ½ cup finely diced celery
- 1 teaspoon salt, plus more to taste
- Freshly ground pepper to taste
- 1 smoked trout, skinned and filleted, each fillet halved lengthwise and crosswise
- 1 ½ teaspoons chopped fresh sage

Direction

- Heat 1 teaspoon of butter in a large heavy skillet over medium-high heat. Add the onions and saute until caramelized, about 10 minutes. Place the onions in a large pot. Add the remaining butter and the apples to the skillet. Saute until caramelized, about 10 minutes. Add the apples to the pot. Pour the sherry into the skillet and cook, scraping the pan with a wooden spoon, about 1 minute. Add this liquid and the water to the pot.
- Bring to a boil, reduce heat and simmer 1 hour 15 minutes. Strain through a fine-mesh sieve. Place in a medium saucepan and add the vegetables. Simmer until tender, about 20 minutes. Season with salt and pepper and ladle among 4 shallow bowls. Place 2 pieces of the trout in each bowl, overlapping them slightly at one end. Sprinkle with sage and serve.

Nutrition Information

- 194: calories;
- 21 grams: sugars;
- 1 gram: monounsaturated fat;
- 0 grams: polyunsaturated fat;
- 38 grams: carbohydrates;
- 8 grams: dietary fiber;
- 4 grams: protein;
- 671 milligrams: sodium;
- 3 grams: fat;

70. Spiced Caramel Syrup

Serving: Enough to top 6 custards | Prep: | Cook: | Ready in: 10mins

Ingredients

- ½ cup (100 grams) sugar
- 10 black peppercorns
- 4 whole cloves
- 1 slice nutmeg (about 1/4 of a whole nutmeg)
- 1 1-inch piece fresh ginger, peeled
- ¼ cup (60 milliliters) water

Direction

- Pour the sugar into a heavy-bottomed medium saucepan set over medium-high heat. Once the sugar starts to color, swirl the pan so that it melts and colors evenly.
- When the caramel is a light reddish-brown color, or as Mr. Skurnick says, "Irish-setter red" (it takes about 5 minutes to reach this stage), drop in the spices and, standing away from the pan, carefully pour in the water. When it boils, reduce the heat to very low and cook for 2 minutes.
- Strain the caramel into a heatproof container (discard the spices or use them for tea), and cool completely. You can keep the syrup covered in the refrigerator for up to 1 week. It will thicken; warm gently to reliquefy.

71. Spiced Pumpkin Creme Brulee With Ginger Dusted Churros

Serving: 6 servings | Prep: | Cook: | Ready in: 1hours15mins

Ingredients

- Crème Brulee
- 3 cups heavy cream
- 1 cup milk
- 1 vanilla bean
- ½ teaspoon cinnamon
- ½ teaspoon allspice
- ¼ teaspoon dried ginger
- ⅔ cup (5 ounces) sugar
- 20 egg yolks
- 1 cup pumpkin puree
- Ginger-Dusted Churros
- Oil for deep frying
- 2 cups water
- 2 cups milk
- 1 pinch salt
- 2 tablespoons sugar
- 4 cups all-purpose flour
- 4 egg whites, beaten
- 1 ounce candied ginger

Direction

- Preheat oven to 325 degrees Fahrenheit. In a saucepan, combine cream, milk, vanilla bean and spices and bring to a simmer.
- In a separate bowl, whisk sugar into egg yolks until fully incorporated. Slowly whisk egg mixture into hot liquid until fully incorporated. Whisk in pumpkin puree.
- Pour the mixture into ramekins or a brulee mold. Place the ramekins in a cake or baking pan, and add enough hot water to the pan to come halfway up the sides of the ramekins. Bake in water bath until custard is set, about 45 minutes.
- Meanwhile, prepare the churros. Preheat oil in a fryer to 375 degrees. In a saucepan, combine water, milk, salt and sugar and bring to a boil. Whisk flour into the mixture in small batches until fully incorporated. Remove from heat and add the egg whites, mixing until the texture is completely smooth.
- Using a pastry bag fitted with a churro tip, pipe the batter into the hot oil in 2-inch strips and fry until golden brown. Drain on paper towel, and roll hot churros in chopped candied ginger and granulated ginger.
- To serve the brulee: Sprinkle top with granulated sugar and caramelize with a torch. Serve with churros.

Nutrition Information

- 1156: calories;
- 24 grams: monounsaturated fat;
- 43 grams: sugars;
- 6 grams: polyunsaturated fat;
- 112 grams: carbohydrates;
- 4 grams: dietary fiber;
- 25 grams: protein;
- 210 milligrams: sodium;
- 68 grams: fat;
- 35 grams: saturated fat;
- 0 grams: trans fat;

72. Spicy Spaghetti With Caramelized Onions And Herbs

Serving: 3 to 4 servings | Prep: | Cook: |Ready in: 45mins

Ingredients

- Kosher salt, as needed
- ¼ cup extra-virgin olive oil
- 2 large white or Spanish onions, halved and very thinly sliced
- 12 ounces spaghetti
- 6 garlic cloves
- ½ teaspoon chile paste or red-pepper flakes, or to taste
- 2 anchovies, chopped (optional)
- 1 cup chopped mix of parsley and basil (or use all parsley)
- ⅓ cup chopped cured Moroccan or other intensely flavored black olives
- 2 tablespoons unsalted butter, cubed
- Lemon wedges, for squeezing
- Grated Parmesan, for serving (optional)

Direction

- Put a large pot of heavily salted water on and let it come to a boil.
- Meanwhile, cook the onions: Heat 1/4 cup oil in a 12-inch skillet over medium heat. Add onions and cook, stirring occasionally, until tender and pale golden at the edges, 20 to 25 minutes. Lower heat if the edges start to brown too quickly or raise heat if onions aren't turning golden quickly enough.
- When the water comes to a boil, cook spaghetti according to package directions until just al dente. Reserve 1 cup pasta water; drain pasta.
- Thinly slice 4 garlic cloves, and stir into golden onions, along with red-pepper flakes. Continue to cook until onions are a rich brown, about 10 minutes longer. If the garlic starts to burn, lower the heat.
- Finely grate remaining garlic cloves, and mash into anchovies using the flat side of your knife. Move some of the onion mixture to the side of the pan and add anchovy paste to bare spot in the skillet. Cook paste for 1 minute, then add herbs and olives, stir everything together, and cook another 1 minute.
- Stir in cooked pasta, butter, and salt to taste, tossing to coat pasta. Add pasta water if it looks dry. Serve with a generous squeeze of lemon, and sprinkle with Parmesan and more chile on top, if desired.

Nutrition Information

- 536: calories;
- 5 grams: sugars;
- 479 milligrams: sodium;
- 22 grams: fat;
- 12 grams: monounsaturated fat;
- 73 grams: carbohydrates;
- 13 grams: protein;
- 6 grams: saturated fat;
- 0 grams: trans fat;
- 2 grams: polyunsaturated fat;

73. Sweet Potato Soup

Serving: 8 servings | Prep: | Cook: |Ready in: 1hours

Ingredients

- 2 ounces (1/2 stick) unsalted butter
- 1 large clove garlic, minced
- 1 medium-size onion, diced
- 1 medium-size carrot, peeled and diced
- 1 rib celery, peeled and diced
- 1 sprig fresh thyme, leaves only
- 1 ¼ pounds sweet potatoes, peeled and diced
- 1 ¼ pounds tart apples, peeled and diced
- 12 ounces Belgian style white beer
- 1 cinnamon stick
- Salt and ground black pepper
- ½ teaspoon ground nutmeg
- 1 cup heavy cream
- 40 mini-marshmallows

Direction

- Melt the butter in a 4-quart saucepan. Add the garlic, onion, carrot and celery and cook on low until tender and translucent. Add the thyme. Add the sweet potatoes, increase the heat a little and cook, stirring from time to time, until the sweet potatoes are tender and start to caramelize, about 12 minutes. Add the apples and cook another 5 minutes or so, until they are tender. Pour in the beer and deglaze the pan.
- Add 5 cups water and the cinnamon stick and simmer for 30 minutes. Season with salt and pepper. Allow soup to cool slightly, then purée it in a blender. You may have to do this in two batches.
- Return the soup to the pot, stir in the nutmeg and cream and simmer for 15 minutes. Check seasonings.
- Thread the marshmallows on several bamboo skewers, leaving a little space between them. Ignite them over a flame, just a few seconds, so they're lightly toasted. Blow out the flame and gently remove the marshmallows to a cutting board. Pour the soup into bowls, top each with a few toasted marshmallows and serve.

Nutrition Information

- 288: calories;
- 12 grams: sugars;
- 17 grams: fat;
- 11 grams: saturated fat;
- 5 grams: dietary fiber;
- 30 grams: carbohydrates;
- 581 milligrams: sodium;
- 0 grams: trans fat;
- 1 gram: polyunsaturated fat;
- 3 grams: protein;

74. Thyme Meringue Cookies With Boozy Apple

Serving: Makes about 3 dozen | Prep: | Cook: |Ready in: 1hours

Ingredients

- For the boozy apple
- ½ firm apple, like Golden Delicious, peeled and cored, sliced into 1/2-inch pieces
- 2 ½ tablespoons bourbon (like Maker's Mark)
- 1 tablespoon organic dark brown sugar
- 1 tablespoon apple-cider vinegar
- For the cookies
- ⅓ cup chopped walnuts
- ¾ cup powdered sugar
- 1 teaspoon fresh thyme leaves
- 2 large egg whites, at room temperature
- ⅛ teaspoon cream of tartar
- Pinch of sea salt
- 1 tablespoon cane sugar
- ½ teaspoon vanilla extract

Direction

-
-

Nutrition Information

- 24: calories;
- 0 grams: protein;

- 4 grams: carbohydrates;
- 3 grams: sugars;
- 7 milligrams: sodium;
- 1 gram: polyunsaturated fat;

75. Vidalia Onion Soup With Wild Rice And Maytag Blue Cheese Croutons

Serving: 4 servings | Prep: | Cook: | Ready in: 1hours15mins

Ingredients

- ½ cup wild rice
- 4 tablespoons unsalted butter
- 2 ½ pounds (about 4) Vidalia onions, or other sweet onions, quartered and very thinly sliced
- 6 cups chicken or vegetable stock
- 3 tablespoons chopped basil
- 3 tablespoons chopped chives
- 4 tablespoons chopped tarragon
- 3 tablespoons chopped flat-leaf parsley
- Salt
- pepper
- 8 slices baguette
- 2 tablespoons extra-virgin olive oil
- 4 ounces Maytag or other young, not too sharp, blue cheese, at room temperature

Direction

- In a small saucepan, combine the rice with 2 cups water. Bring to a boil, then reduce heat to low. Cover and simmer until the rice is tender and the water is absorbed, 45 to 60 minutes.
- Meanwhile, place a wide, deep pot over medium heat. Melt the butter and add the onions, tossing them until wilted and well coated. Cook the onions, turning them with a spatula every 5 to 10 minutes, until soft and browned but not burned; this may take 30 to 40 minutes.
- Add the stock and simmer for 20 minutes. Wrap the herbs in a small piece of cheesecloth and tie with kitchen string. Drop the bundle into the broth for 1 minute, then remove it. Season to taste with salt and pepper.
- Heat oven to 400 degrees. Brush both sides of the baguette slices with oil. Bake on a baking sheet until light golden brown, 12 to 15 minutes. While the croutons are still warm, spread them with blue cheese.
- To serve, divide the rice among four bowls, and ladle broth and onions on top. Float 2 croutons in the center of each bowl, and sprinkle with more pepper.

Nutrition Information

- 621: calories;
- 12 grams: monounsaturated fat;
- 3 grams: polyunsaturated fat;
- 63 grams: carbohydrates;
- 5 grams: dietary fiber;
- 1730 milligrams: sodium;
- 32 grams: fat;
- 15 grams: saturated fat;
- 0 grams: trans fat;
- 22 grams: sugars;
- 23 grams: protein;

Index

A

Apple 3,4,16,30,33,53,56

Apricot 3,5

B

Bacon 3,11,39

Banana 3,5

Beans 39

Black pepper 19,35,50

Bread 3,34

Broth 4,53

Buckwheat 3,8

Butter 3,10,11,16,28,37,42,48

C

Cake 3,13,36,42

Caramel 1,3,4,5,7,11,13,14,15,16,17,18,19,20,21,23,29,31,33,34,37,39,40,48,52,53,54,55

Cauliflower 3,47

Cayenne pepper 30

Champ 11

Chard 3,34,40

Cheese 3,4,25,39,57

Cherry 8

Chicken 3,7,21

Chocolate 3,5

Coconut 3,23

Cognac 20

Crab 3,32

Cream 3,5,8,10,28,31,36,42

Crumble 49

D

Duck 3,4,25,52

F

Fennel 3,7,41

Fig 3,17,39

Flour 30,38,39

Fruit 3,24,31

G

Garlic 3,34

Gin 4,24,54

Gorgonzola 39,40

Grapes 3,12

H

Herbs 4,55

Honey 3,5,17,27,30

L

Leek 3,18

Lemon 3,35,55

Ling 3,32

M

Mango 3,28

Marmalade 3,25

Mascarpone 15

Matzo 3,19,33

Meat 3,32,46

Meringue 4,56

Mint 7

Mushroom 3,19,21

N

Nut 3,5,6,7,8,9,10,11,12,13,14,15,16,17,18,19,20,21,22,23,24,25,26,27,28,29,30,31,32,33,34,35,36,37,38,39,40,42,43,44,4

5,46,47,48,49,50,51,52,53,55,56,57

O

Oatmeal 3,31

Oil 27,54

Onion 3,4,11,18,19,21,23,25,26,34,39,40,41,42,53,55,57

Orange 3,4,7,9,47,52

P

Parmesan 11,12,26,40,41,49,55

Pasta 3,34,35

Peach 3,20,29,36,37,50

Pear 3,14,38,42

Peel 7,9,14,27,28,42,48

Pepper 3,8,12,28

Pie 3,30,38

Pineapple 3,23,38,39

Pizza 3,39,40,41,42

Pomegranate 3,4,38,52

Pork 3,22

Potato 4,55

Praline 3,27,41,42

Pulse 32

Pumpkin 3,4,43,48,54

Q

Quinoa 3,50

R

Rabbit 3,25

Rice 3,4,16,57

Ricotta 3,40

Rigatoni 3,47

Rosemary 3,9

Rum 46

S

Salad 3,26

Salt 3,12,15,18,19,21,26,29,30,32,37,40,41,43,47,48,49,50,56,57

Sausage 3,49

Scallop 3,51

Sea salt 8,15,29

Seeds 53

Shallot 3,11

Sorbet 3,28

Soup 4,55,57

Spaghetti 4,55

Spinach 3,11,23

Squash 3,11

Stuffing 3,23

Sugar 3,10,33

Swiss chard 8,9,34,35

Syrup 3,4,15,54

T

Tabasco 51

Thyme 3,4,17,30,56

Tomato 46

Trout 4,53

V

Vegetable oil 30,49

Vegetarian 3,44

W

Walnut 4,52

Wine 3,7

Z

Zest 16,32

L

lasagna 12

Conclusion

Thank you again for downloading this book!

I hope you enjoyed reading about my book!

If you enjoyed this book, please take the time to share your thoughts and post a review on Amazon. It'd be greatly appreciated!

Write me an honest review about the book – I truly value your opinion and thoughts and I will incorporate them into my next book, which is already underway.

Thank you!

If you have any questions, **feel free to contact at:** author@thymerecipes.com

Maria Bingham

thymerecipes.com

Printed in Great Britain
by Amazon